Handbook
for
TEACHING SECONDARY SCHOOL SOCIAL STUDIES

James W. Stockard, Jr.
Louisiana State University

Long Grove, Illinois

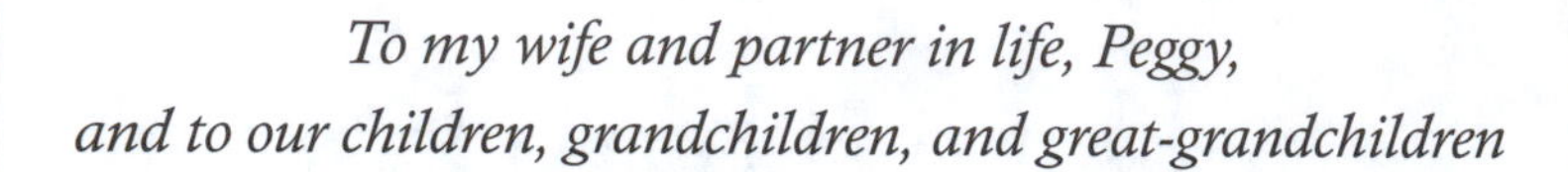

To my wife and partner in life, Peggy,
and to our children, grandchildren, and great-grandchildren

For information about this book, contact:
Waveland Press, Inc.
4180 IL Route 83, Suite 101
Long Grove, IL 60047-9580
(847) 634-0081
info@waveland.com
www.waveland.com

10-digit ISBN 1-57766-454-X
13-digit ISBN 978-1-57766-454-3

Printed in the United States of America

8 7 6 5 4 3 2

Contents

Section V
The Comprehensive Curriculum and Content Standards 95

Section VI
Basic Instructional Considerations 127

Preface

Revitalizing the social studies curriculum in secondary school classrooms encourages students to become caring, vibrant citizens who make informed decisions. The *Handbook for Teaching Secondary School Social Studies* is a guide, a tool, and a reference for helping pre-service and in-service teachers clarify their vision regarding the most effective ways to teach social studies in secondary school classrooms. It will help teachers to become creative practitioners who can motivate students; create stimulating learning environments; and bring history, geography, economics, and political science to life. It will, in effect, help teachers make social scientists of their students.

The handbook is brief and manageable, yet it provides pre-service and in-service teachers with comprehensive and in-depth coverage of research-based pedagogy, planning skills, standards-based instructional-delivery approaches, and grade-level expectations for the core disciplines of the social studies. The information contained in this book will enable teachers to become the catalyst for students' transformation into cognizant, confident citizens capable of making a difference in our world.

Introduction

Even though we are well into the twenty-first century, our high schools remain organized on twentieth-century needs and expectations. What, then, can we do to ensure that all students graduate from high school prepared to succeed in the twenty-first century?

We must understand that there have been fundamental shifts in our economic situation, creating an economy so new that we barely understand it, and yet we must devise new ways of educating our high school students to succeed in this new economy. Globalization, technological advances, and demographic shifts have changed our economy. Instead of an economy that supports a middle class with standardized factory routines and tasks that flourish unopposed, our workers now must be prepared to seek solutions to new and complicated problems, engage in higher-order thinking skills, and be competitive with workers on a worldwide basis. Our high schools now must provide young people with a new set of skills in order to succeed in this new economy—a set of skills different from the ones around which we have organized our educational system in the past.

In that regard, we must look at our traditional structures and patterns of high school education and understand that they may be holding us back from achieving our twenty-first century goals and aspirations. Making changes in these structures and patterns often goes against some of our deepest, most fundamental and revered beliefs about secondary education. We must ask and seek solutions to questions such as, "What do our students need to know and be able to do in the new economy?" and "When it comes to educating our young people, what changes does our experience tell us we must make?"

The changing nature of the workforce creates new demands on our educational system. Every worker must be innovative and think critically. They must solve new problems, utilize technology, and communicate well. Students must have a deep foundation of factual knowledge to develop competence in an area of inquiry. They need to understand facts and ideas in the context of a conceptual framework. It is important that they learn to organize knowledge in ways that facilitate retrieval and application. Students need to understand, control, and manipulate their own cognitive processes; to become "metacognitive"—to learn how to learn. Future issues in education will be driven by four exponents, all of which will affect teachers (Houlihan, 2005):

Demographic Considerations

- Poverty rates for children have doubled and are highest in the industrial world.
- Poverty rates for the elderly have been cut in half.
- Twenty-five percent of the population is elderly and expecting government benefits.
- One out of four households has school-age children.
- The number of single-parent households is rising.
- The number of married couples is declining.

Who will support our schools? Who will pay for quality education? How do we reach out to others?

Economic Considerations

- For every new computer programming job created in 2005, four new janitorial jobs were generated.
- The "offshore" phenomenon will increase.

To keep pace with economic changes, our only hope lies in skill development.

- Spending habits increase with age; the peak spending age is 46.5.
- Ninety-five percent of spending is nondiscretionary.
- Some pension funds having serious deficits (General Motors, for example).

What will be the impact on school funding?

Political Considerations

- One-third of the electorate is over age 65.
- One-half of the U.S. population lives in 10 states (CA, TX, FL, GA, IL, PA, NY, NJ, MI, OH).
- Health care costs are exploding.
- Pension costs are exploding.
- A 40% increase in productivity is necessary just to keep up with demand.
- People age 65 and over receive 11 times more per person in federal spending than do children under 18.

Global Considerations

- In 1700, just over 300 years ago, the world's population was 400 million.

- In 1880, the population of the world had grown to 1 billion.
- In 1950, it was 3 billion.
- Today, the population of the world is over 6 billion people.
- The most populated regions of the world are East Asia (China and Japan, 1.5 billion); South Asia (India, 1 billion); and Indonesia (Java and surrounding areas 2 billion). Some 4.5 billion people live in these areas.
- Every second person in the world is Asian.

The World from Another Perspective

If we could shrink the Earth's population to a village of precisely 100 people, with all of the existing human ratios remaining the same, it would look something like the following.[1]

- Fifty-seven would be Asian.
- Twenty-one would be European.
- Fourteen would be from the Western Hemisphere, both north and south.
- Eight would be African.
- Fifty-two would be female.
- Forty-eight would be male.
- Seventy would be nonwhite.
- Thirty would be white.
- Seventy would be non-Christian.
- Thirty would be Christian.
- Eighty-nine would be heterosexual.
- Eleven would be homosexual.
- Six people would possess 59% of the entire world's wealth, and all six would be from the United States.
- Eighty would live in substandard housing.
- Seventy would be unable to read.
- Fifty would suffer from malnutrition.
- One would be near death; 1 would be near birth.
- One (yes, only 1) would have a college education.
- One would own a computer.

Work is different, tools are different, communication is different, information is different, kids are different, learning is different—so teaching must be different. How does education need to change? The following table indicates some of the traditional teaching models and how they will change to meet the new learning environments facing the United States.

New Teachers Will Face New Learning Environments

Traditional	New
Teacher-centered instruction	Learner-centered instruction
Single-sense stimulus	Multisensory stimulus
Single-path progression	Multipath progression
Single media	Multimedia; hypermedia
Isolated work	Collaborative work
Information delivery	Information exchange
Passive learning	Active, exploratory, inquiry-based learning
Factual, literal thinking	Critical thinking; informed decision making
Reactive response	Proactive, planned action
Isolated, artificial context	Authentic, real-world context

As we contemplate the new learning environments facing new teachers, it is important to contrast the traditional with new instructional delivery methods. We must look at our educational philosophies and peek at the historical context of education in America. In that regard, the following section will examine the importance of a teacher's personal philosophy, followed by a section briefly depicting the history of education in America.

Note

[1] Attributed source: Phillip M. Harter, MD, FACEP, Stanford University, School of Medicine.

SECTION I

Philosophical and Historical Background

Philosophy of Education

We do not see things as they are… we see things as we are.
—Anais Nin, *U.S. (French-born) author and diarist (1903—1977)*

Over sixty years ago, L. Thomas Hopkins (1941) stressed the importance of a philosophy in the practice of teaching and schooling when he said, "Philosophy has entered into every important decision that has ever been made about curriculum and teaching in the past and will continue to be the basis of every important decision in the future" (p. 198). Hopkins was right. Philosophy is pervasive in the educational process. It determines which knowledge we hold worthwhile, which values we embrace, and which decisions we make as educational practitioners.

Developing Your Philosophy of Education

Often, when a newly certified teacher applies for a teaching position, the hiring entity (e.g., the principal, superintendent, personnel director) will ask the prospective teacher to write a description of his or her philosophy of education. In reviewing various educational philosophies, you may find yourself in agreement with certain beliefs and viewpoints held by the various philosophies and in disagreement with others. Such a stance is very common and can still yield a consistent viewpoint. Often, we call a point of view that is derived from a combination of two or more viewpoints an *eclectic* philosophy. In today's world of education that has seen so many innovations, changes, variations, movements, and fads, a majority of educators seem to have an eclectic philosophy of education, one that contains elements and permutations from several philosophies. In that regard, it may be enlightening to investigate your own educational viewpoints.

The Self-Test on Educational Views[1]

The following educational statements cover almost all aspects of the educational enterprise. They are arranged to express points of view from the essentialist (conservative) or progressive (liberal) educational philosophies. By recording the statements with which you have strong agreement, you can get a good idea about your own philosophy of education. Take the self-test and discover how your own personal philosophy of education may be characterized.

Instructions for the Self-Test. Make a check mark next to the statements with which you agree strongly. (Do not check a statement unless you *strongly* agree.) Then, using the key at the end of the self-test, place an "E" for essentialism or a "P" for progressivism next to your check-marked numerals, and add the number of E's and the number of P's. If there are over twenty E's, there is a likelihood that you lean strongly toward an essentialist (conservative) philosophy of education. If there are over twenty P's, you are more likely to be of the progressive (liberal) persuasion in your philosophical views of education. If neither a conservative (E) nor liberal (P) result prevails, you are probably an eclectic in your educational views. Although not scientifically based, this exercise may be fairly accurate in predicting your overall educational viewpoint.

The Self-Test

1. Despite community opposition, school teachers have the moral and legal right to teach about sensitive issues.
2. Parents should be consulted periodically about acceptable educational methodology because they help pay for schools.
3. Social studies classes should stress free enterprise and the right economic system.
4. In secondary schools particularly, social criticism is a function of public education.
5. The major societal function of the school is to teach youth to read, write, and compute well at all school levels.
6. Liberal arts education and vocational education are of equal importance.
7. Marketable vocational skills must be a fundamental function of the school.
8. Social problems should not be a significant focus of the school.
9. Discipline that is externally enforced and humane leads to self-discipline.
10. Promotion to the next grade is usually justifiable despite academic progress.
11. Progress reflected on report cards should be from many points of view: academic, social, emotional, and physical.
12. The concept of "truth" is relative.
13. The concept of "truth" is absolute, either in terms of the accumulated wisdom of the ages or of divine revelation.
14. Change is the only social constant or absolute.
15. Subject-matter relevance is determined chiefly by the intellectual desires of learners or by present social problems.
16. For students who are not science majors, general science is a more appropriate subject for study than chemistry, physics, and the like.
17. Students should be evaluated on how well they compare with others in most subjects, because life is competitive.
18. It may take years to realize the usefulness of formal study.
19. Students should be taught that learning is frequently painful.
20. Children's experiences inside the school must be closely related to their life experiences outside the school.
21. By and large, effort generates interest.
22. By and large, interest generates effort.
23. Voluntary prayer should be allowed in U.S. public schools.

(continued)

24. Racial desegregation should not be ambitiously pursued until better housing and equal employment opportunities become a reality for all.
25. Rather than memorization of facts, critical thinking should dominate the teaching approaches in elementary school social studies.
26. We can measure an idea's value only by its immediate usefulness.
27. By and large, requiring all college students to study a foreign language is a waste of time.
28. When school budgets are restricted, curtailing driver education, home economics, and varsity sports should precede reductions in the sciences and humanities.
29. To provide gifted students with as much challenge as possible, ability grouping is necessary.
30. Adjustments should be made in college admissions tests to permit more students to enroll.
31. With a few exceptions, most American colleges and universities do not deserve the label of "institution of higher education," because they are primarily centers of vocational education.
32. Most high school subjects of study should be elective.
33. At the elementary level, teacher education should focus more on what to teach rather than on how to teach.
34. As an educational activity, reading has no equal at any level of schooling.
35. Reading is but one important avenue among the many arteries leading to the acquisition of knowledge.
36. Transmitting the cultural heritage is the basic purpose of formal education.
37. Nurturing the development of the total personality is the basic purpose of formal education.
38. A primary goal of K–12 education should be individualized instruction.
39. The quality of mutually shared experiences gives rise to morality.
40. The concept of the *whole child* is meaningless, since ways to define and evaluate a "whole" child are vague.
41. If indoctrination can exist at all in the public school, it must be in how to pursue knowledge.
42. Problem solving should be employed whenever possible.
43. Instead of approaching the study of accumulated wisdom chronologically, it should be studied topically in light of relevance.
44. Vocational subjects will never enjoy the same educational prestige as mathematics and the sciences.
45. At all grade levels, students should be taught the difference between work and play.
46. Valuable time is taken away from the basic subjects when we teach sex education, career education, African-American studies, and the like.
47. Teachers and pupils should jointly determine pupil conformity to classroom rules.
48. The dominant authority figure in the classroom should be the teacher.
49. Direction by a strong, humane authority figure is what most students need.

50. Experience in group activities leads to self-discipline.
51. Corporal punishment is not a humane method of classroom control.
52. In order to retain a professional image, teachers should remain emotionally distant from students.
53. School discipline should be permissive, within broad limitations, so that students might learn social skills through group participation.
54. In light of limited financial resources, individualized instruction is unrealistic.
55. Teaching has always been more of an art than a science and always will be.
56. An elementary teacher can feel successful if a pupil makes strides in social and emotional maturity during the school year but fails to make significant academic progress.
57. The teacher's will should prevail if a student disagrees on what should be learned in an independent study project.
58. The teacher's authority should not be undermined by influence exerted on students by the school counselor.
59. School dress codes are necessary.
60. By and large, knowledge about the structure of the federal government will make students better citizens.
61. The more students learn to perform tasks by memory, the more they can think productively about similar and more complicated topics.
62. A passion for a socially acceptable standard can be a religious experience.
63. To believe in moral absolutes and practice experimental methods in teaching is of small concern.
64. It matters little what approach the teacher uses if students like school and are succeeding.
65. Because there is some truth in all viewpoints, frequent discourse about how bad traditional educational methods have been becomes tiresome.
66. Classroom methodology does not necessarily need to reflect a teacher's ethical beliefs.
67. It is always good to have reform movements at work in education to prevent stagnation.
68. Reports of pupil progress should reflect social and emotional growth as well as growth in academic achievement.

Key for the Self-Test on Educational Views

1. P	10. P	19. E	28. E	37. P	46. E	55. E	64. N
2. E	11. P	20. P	29. E	38. P	47. P	56. P	65. N
3. E	12. P	21. E	30. P	39. P	48. E	57. E	66. N
4. P	13. E	22. P	31. E	40. E	49. E	58. E	67. N
5. E	14. P	23. E	32. P	41. P	50. P	59. E	68. N
6. P	15. P	24. E	33. E	42. P	51. P	60. E	
7. P	16. P	25. P	34. E	43. P	52. E	61. E	
8. E	17. E	26. P	35. P	44. E	53. P	62. P	
9. E	18. E	27. P	36. E	45. E	54. N	63. N	

Writing a Statement of Your Philosophy of Education

Using the results of the self-test, you can transform some of the statements with which you have close agreement into a document describing your own personal philosophy of education. Remember, when you go for an interview for employment as a teacher, the interviewers will often ask you to write a brief statement of your philosophy of education. In that regard, it is an excellent idea to practice writing a statement of your personal philosophy of education ahead of time. Your statement about your philosophy is often used by administrators to judge whether you, as an applicant, are the kind of person that patrons of the school system would want teaching their students.

Here are a few suggestions for writing your own personal philosophy of education:

- Be positive; don't talk about the problems in education but rather talk about how you will make a difference.
- Your educational philosophy should reflect your own approach to education, and it should be based on your personal beliefs and show the influence of college work, readings, and thinkers. In that regard, it is appropriate to "drop names" in your philosophy; for example, you might say, "Like Dewey, I believe in the pragmatic, hands-on, student-participatory approach of learning by doing." Be sure, however, that you understand the philosophy of the person whose name you "drop" since you might be questioned about it in your interview.
- Your statement of philosophy should "look good" (that is, have a neat appearance). If you write it by hand at the interview, be careful about your handwriting. Practice ahead of time so that you will know what you want to write. If you can do it in advance, use a word processor and, in either case, be careful about grammar and spelling.
- Your written philosophy should have an introduction and a conclusion, and your conclusion should provide a logical ending to your philosophy statement.
- Select some of the items from the self-test with which you have strong agreement on educational views and practice rewriting them to fit into your written personal philosophy.
- Finally, be brief; less is more when it comes to making an impression.

History of American Education

The historical foundations of social studies are melded into the history of American education. For that reason, and in that regard, it is good to take a brief review of the history of education in America. In examining the history of American education, we can gain a perspective of the evolving content and subject matter that became the social studies.

During the first 200 years or more, the concern in American education was with the social and economic significance of content and subject matter, a sort of sociology of knowledge. Shaped by the dominant philosophy of perennialism and transcending the early periods of behaviorism and scientism, this sociology of knowledge became firmly established with the rise of progressivism in American educational thinking (Kliebard, 1992). The curriculum is under constant revision, affected by the significant political, social, economic, and cultural context in which it is created. Religious convictions, economic motives, class value systems, political ideologies, and social action, as well as views of the essence of knowledge, all intermingle to form the significant context in which curriculum is decided (Pinar et al., 1995).

The Colonial Period

Settled primarily by Puritans who had come to America for religious reasons, colonial Massachusetts served as the focal point for the historical foundations of education in America from about 1642 through 1776. The Puritans adhered steadfastly to their religious principles. For the Puritans, the purpose of schooling was to teach children to read so that they could read the Bible as well as notices of civil affairs. By and large, the church leaders and the civil leaders were one and the same. Civil law and church law were closely aligned. The principles of the Puritan church and colonial laws were tightly bound together. There was no separation between church and state.

It is not surprising, then, that the Commonwealth of Massachusetts passed a law in 1642 requiring parents and guardians of children to make cer-

Figure 1.1 The Colonial Period

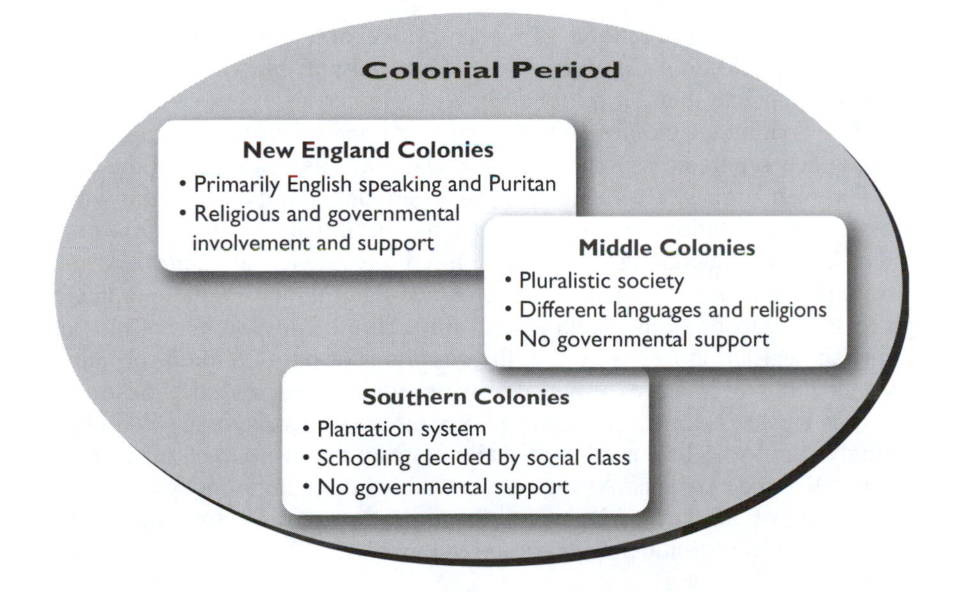

tain that their children could read the Bible and understand the religious principles of the Puritans. This was followed five years later with the Massachusetts Act of 1647 requiring every town of fifty or more families to appoint a teacher of reading and writing. The Act of 1647 was called the "Old Deluder Satan Act," because its purpose was to teach the children to read and understand the Bible so that they could outwit that "old deluder, Satan." Towns of 100 or more families were to engage a teacher of Latin, as well, so that students would be prepared for entry into Harvard College. (Harvard, the first colonial college, was established in Boston in 1636 and had a heavy emphasis on theology and the classics). All of the other New England colonies, except Rhode Island, followed suit. These two pieces of legislation, the Massachusetts Acts of 1642 and 1647, are regarded by most historians as the roots of the public school movement in America (Ornstein & Hunkins, 1998).

Geographically and culturally, the Colonial Period can be divided into three regions: New England, the Middle Colonies, and the Southern Colonies. In New England, about one thousand Puritans settled near Boston in 1630, and towns sprang up. The Puritans led the public school movement in the colonies because they wanted to avoid an illiterate class with dependent poor, reminiscent of the underclass that many of them had left in England and other parts of Europe.

Unlike New England, the Middle Colonies had no common religion or even a common language. The people who settled in the Middle Colonies came from various national backgrounds, like Dutch and Swedish. In addition, they represented many religious groups, such as Puritan, Mennonite, and Catholic. This gave rise to independent and parochial schools which were associated with different ethnic and religious groups. Because of the competition between political and religious groups, the New England idea of district-wide control of schools gave way to local and community control of schools in the Middle Colonies. Ideas about cultural pluralism that many espouse today had their birth in the Middle Colonies.

The Southern Colonies were primarily composed of large plantations, often widely separated from neighbors. Education was a function of the family. The plantation system created a privileged class composed of the white children of plantation owners who had the benefit of private tutors and, often, European schooling. Tutors were hired to come to the plantations and school the youngsters of the plantation owners until they were old enough to go to European boarding schools and universities. The Southern Colonies did enact legislation to ensure that the guardians of poor children, orphans, and illegitimate children provided private educational and/or vocational training. However, for the most part poor whites who worked the soil had no formal education. They usually stayed illiterate and grew up to be subsistence farmers like their parents. At the very bottom of the plantation system were the children of the slaves, relegated to the underclass of the plantation system where they were forbidden to learn to read and write. The political and economic system propagated by the plantations retarded the development of schools in the Southern Colonies and created an educational handicap that was felt long after the Civil War (Ornstein & Levine, 1993).

Despite differences in religious beliefs, language, and economic systems, the family and religious commitment were both high priorities in the socialization and education of all children in the New England Colonies, the Middle Colonies, and the Southern Colonies. Too, despite their regional distinctions and differences, all three colonial regions were strongly influenced by the political concepts of England. The curriculum consisted of reading, writing, and some arithmetic; an inculcation in the rudiments of religious faith; lessons designed to help students become high minded, ethical, and moral; and training in manners and deportment (Beauchamp, 1964).

The Town School. In the New England Colonies, the town school was a standard prototype. A crude, one-room structure dominated by the teacher's lectern at the front of the room and attended by both boys and girls, it was a community school. The town school was locally controlled and the curriculum was focused on reading, writing, and religious dogma. Boys and girls, ranging in age from 5 to 14, sat on benches and studied their assignments. Then, in turn, the schoolmaster would call on each pupil to give a recitation. Attendance was irregular and somewhat haphazard, depending on the weather conditions and the need for children to stay at home to work on the farm (Monroe, 1940). The *dame school* was a low-level primary school usually conducted by an untrained woman in her own home. More often than not, dame schools were conducted by housewives and were found in more rural settings of New England. The town school was, however, the important institution for New England colonial society and paved the way for the concept of community schools.

Parochial and Private Schools. The prevailing schools in the Middle Colonies were parochial and private schools. Ethnic groups, missionary societies, and other religious groups established elementary schools to educate their own children. Like the New England town schools, the primary concentration was on reading, writing, some arithmetic, and the Bible. Being the "melting pot" of colonial America, the Middle Colonies also had many students who received their education through an apprenticeship while learning a trade from a master (Johnson et al., 1999).

The Southern Colonies were a mixture of private schools for the upper-class children and charity schools for the children of the poor. The private schools were oriented, as were the New England town schools and the Middle Colonies parochial schools, to the teaching of reading, writing, arithmetic, and a study of the Bible. The charity schools of the Southern Colonies trained the children of the poor (who were lucky enough to attend) in the three R's and in learning to recite religious hymns (which was not as difficult as studying the Bible).

Latin Grammar Schools. First established in Boston in 1635, the Latin Grammar School was a secondary school devised to prepare the sons of the upper class for entry into Harvard College. The Latin Grammar School was the first permanent school of its type in America, and the idea spread quickly to other colonial towns. Charlestown opened a Latin Grammar School one year later in 1636, and within sixteen years after the Massachusetts Bay Colony had been founded, there were seven or eight towns with Latin Grammar Schools. They catered primarily to those who planned to enter the professions of law, medicine, the ministry, or teaching, or to those who would become the merchants and business owners of the colonies.

Latin and Greek were demanded of students for entry into European colleges, and colonial colleges followed suit. It is little wonder, then, that Latin Grammar Schools, which were designed to prepare students for college, had such a classical and traditional curriculum. There were some courses in Greek, rhetoric, and logic, but probably three-quarters of the curriculum was preparation in Latin with little or no attention given to the other arts and sciences (Brown, 1926). Religion was prevalent both in the atmosphere, with the master regularly leading his students in prayer, and in the exhausting and unexciting regimen of the studies themselves, where regular and thorough quizzes were given on the sermons.

The Latin Grammar School was one of colonial America's closest links to the educational system of Europe. Its course of study resembled the curriculum of the classical humanist schools of the European Renaissance, which supported the religious and social institutions of that era (Spring, 1990). Colleges of the time did not accept females, so girls did not attend the Latin Grammar School. Since only a small percentage of the boys in any one community could hope to attend college, the enrollment in the Latin grammar schools was very low. "As late as 1785 there were only two Latin grammar schools in Boston, and the combined enrollment in these two schools was only sixty-four young men" (Johnson et al., 1999, p. 300).

The Academy. Another institution in America that provided education at the secondary level was the academy. There was a need for more and better-trained skilled workers by the middle of the eighteenth century, and Benjamin Franklin (1706–1790) of Pennsylvania recognized a need for a more practical secondary school. Consequently, his proposal for a new kind of secondary school with a different philosophy, curriculum, and methodology brought about the establishment of the first American Academy in Philadelphia in 1751.

Everything about the academy was geared to preparing young people for employment. Latin was no longer a crucial subject, but rather a diversified curriculum of English grammar, composition, rhetoric, public speaking, and classics was offered. In addition, the study of a foreign language which would be practical and instrumental in one's career was encouraged (a future businessman might study French, German, or Spanish, for example, and a prospective clergyman could study Latin or Greek). History replaced religion as the chief ethical study. The academy also introduced many practical and manual skills into the curriculum (printing, cabinet making, bookkeeping, carpentry, and the like), forming the basis for today's vocational curricula.

The academy departed significantly from the Latin Grammar School and its affinity for European methodologies and became the first truly American educational institution. Similar academies were established throughout America, many admitting girls, and eventually replaced the Latin Grammar School as the predominant American institution for secondary education (Ornstein & Levine, 1993).

The New England Primer. The most widely used textbook in the colonies for over 100 years, the *New England Primer* was, in essence, the first American basal reader. Published in the last decade of the seventeenth century and imbued with moral principles and religious doctrines, the *New England Primer* was used to teach the ABCs through rote memorization and sold more than three million copies. The solemn disposition of the Puritan religious dogma was evident (see photo).

Puritan religious dogma prevails throughout the solemn rhymes featured in the New England Primer.

The Hornbook. An absence of books and writing tools brought into existence a paddle-shaped board with a sheet of parchment covered by a transparent sheath made by peeling and flattening cattle horns. Children used the hornbook to memorize the alphabet, the Lord's Prayer, and the scriptures by sliding sheets of parchment inscribed with the material to be memorized under the transparent sheath, which protected the parchment so that it could be used over and over again in different hornbooks (Ornstein & Levine, 1993).

The National Period

A new era in education began to emerge prior to the American Revolution and continued into the *national period*, from about 1776 through 1850. It was characterized by the linkage of free public schooling with political freedom and popular government. The great documents of the time, the Declaration of Independence, the Bill of Rights, and the Northwest Ordinances, emphasized liberty and equality through free public education. In 1785, for example, these ordinances created townships in the Northwest Territory and reserved the sixteenth section of each township for the purpose of public schooling. Thanks to these ordinances, 39 states acquired over 154 million acres of land from the federal government for schools (Cubberley, 1947).

Benjamin Rush (1745–1813). Rush theorized that emphasizing a curriculum dominated by the classics, Latin, and Greek made the common people prejudicial toward institutions of learning. Universal education had no chance with Latin and Greek reigning over the curriculum. To spend four or five years learning two dead languages, speculated Rush, was foolish. He felt that if the time committed to Latin and Greek were instead devoted to science, "the human condition would be much improved" (Rush, 1786, p. 29).

Ever the pragmatist, Rush devised an educational plan for Pennsylvania and the country, advocating free elementary schools in every township where there were 100 or more families, free academies in each county, and free colleges and universities in each state. Rush contended that a system of free schools would create such a productive workforce and entrepreneurial citizenry that it would not only pay for the educational system but eventually even lower taxes. Rush's curriculum, of course, was absent Latin and Greek and emphasized reading, writing, and arithmetic in the elementary school; the sciences, arts, English, and German in secondary school and college; and high morals and good manners throughout the educational program (Rush, 1786).

Thomas Jefferson (1743–1826). A basic assumption of Thomas Jefferson was that the state had a responsibility to foster and nurture an educated citizenry in order to ensure a liberated, democratic society. Jefferson, himself a man of wide-ranging interests that embraced science, agriculture, politics, and education, advocated a broad education for everyone, both the common people and the landed gentry, at state expense.

Jefferson's proposal divided Virginia's counties into wards with free elementary schools that would teach reading, writing, arithmetic, and history. At the secondary level, Jefferson proposed twenty grammar schools where poor students who demonstrated academic promise would be provided scholarships. The secondary program would consist of Latin, Greek, English, mathematics, and geography. After successfully completing grammar school, half of the scholarship students would be assigned to teach in the elementary schools and the ten with the highest academic achievement would attend the College of William and Mary. The idea of equality of educational opportunity for the poor as well as the use of the lower schools to identify bright students for extended educational opportunities were Jeffersonian concepts.

Noah Webster (1758–1843). The American people had declared political independence from England by their act of revolution in 1776, so when the Constitution became the law of the land in 1789, Noah Webster proposed that Americans should also declare their cultural independence from England. Believing that a distinctive national language and literature would promote a sense of national identity,

> . . . Webster set out to reshape the English language used in the United States. He believed that a uniquely American language would (1) eliminate the remains of European usage, (2) create a uniform American speech that would be free of localism and provincialism, and (3) promote self-conscious American cultural nationalism. (Ornstein & Levine, 1993, p. 68)

To Webster, language acquisition was directly related to organized education, and as children learned a distinctive American language, they would also begin to act and think like Americans. A distinctively American language would become the semantic adhesive of national union, Webster reasoned. In that regard, he felt that a distinctively American language would also have to be phonically simple so that it would be appropriate for everyone, especially the common people.

> The American language that Webster proposed would have to be taught deliberately and systematically to the young in the nation's schools. Because the curriculum of these Americanized schools would be shaped by the books that the students read, Webster spent much of his life writing spelling and reading books. His *Grammatical Institute of the English Language* was published in 1783. The first part of the *Institute* was later printed as *The American Spelling Book*, which was widely used throughout the United States in the first half of the nineteenth century. Webster's spelling book went through many editions; it is estimated that 15 million copies had been sold by 1837. Webster's great work was *The American Dictionary*, which was completed in 1825 after twenty-five years of laborious research. Often termed the "schoolmaster of the Republic," Noah Webster was an educational statesman of the early national period whose work helped to create a sense of American language, identity, and nationality. (Ornstein & Levine, 1993, p. 68)

William Holmes McGuffey (1800–1873). William Holmes McGuffey, an Ohio educator, wrote a series of five graded reading books, simply called the *Readers*, which were the most popular textbooks of the period and paved the way for the graded school system that emerged in 1840s America. Acknowledging America's cultural indebtedness to Europe and the English contributions to American education relative to art, science, literature, law, and proper manners, McGuffey showed how America had made its own distinctive moral and political contributions to humankind by the full realization of social promise for the common people.

First published in 1836, the five *McGuffey Readers* sold more than 120 million copies by 1920. McGuffey's readers successfully combined the virtues of the Protestant faith with rural America's virtuous living and belief in hard work, patriotism, diligence, and heroism. Through his *Readers*, McGuffey brought several generations of Americans into accord with patriotism and a high regard for home, the church, honest work, and good citizenship (Westerhoff, 1978).

Horace Mann (1796–1859). As secretary of the Massachusetts State Board of Education, Horace Mann was one of the movers and shakers of the educational awakening that took place in America between 1820 and 1860. As secretary, Mann was instrumental in the development of Massachusetts' common elementary schools, which were designed to provide a basic elementary education for all children. In addition, Mann was able to keep this breakthrough progress as well as other pertinent educational issues before the public by publishing one of America's earliest professional educational periodicals, *The Common School Journal*. Perhaps one effect of the *Journal* was that the first compulsory elementary school attendance law in the country was passed by the Massachusetts legislature in 1852, and by the year 1900 similar compulsory education laws were passed by 32 other states (Johnson et al., 1999).

European Educational Influences

The schools in America from the Colonial Period and through most of the National Period were characterized by motives, curriculum, and administration that were primarily religious. School was viewed as an unpleasant place with harsh discipline. The teaching and learning was formal, impersonal, and conducted primarily by rote memorization. Students were constantly exhorted to do their work and admonished when they did not learn. Although American politicians had leveled much criticism toward European thinking, American educational reformers were greatly influenced by European educational concepts.

Johan Heinrich Pestalozzi (1746–1827). The Swiss educator ". . . Pestalozzi, probably more than any other educational reformer, laid the basis for the modern elementary school and helped to reform elementary-school practice" (Knight, 1951, p. 512). Pestalozzianism revolved around the concept that children learn through the senses rather than with words. The emphasis was on teaching children via objects and firsthand experiences and treating them with understanding, patience, and love. Providing the children with emotional security through affection and trust while appealing to the auditory and visual senses were major tenets of the Pestalozzian methodology. Today's emphasis on the concepts of hands-on, student-participatory, and learning-by-doing is the product of Pestalozzi's influence (concepts later embraced and endorsed by John Dewey).

Johann Fredrich Herbart (1776–1841). Imported into the United States by students from the Bloomington Normal School in Illinois who encountered the ideas of Herbart while studying in Germany, Herbartianism introduced a formal system of organization into teaching. This attempt to make a science out of teaching was sorely needed by the elementary schools of the day because they were often disorganized and lacking in methodology. Herbart advocated the following formal steps in the teaching process:

1. *Preparation*, in which previous learning experiences and readiness of the learner are considered. (The teacher asks, What do my students know? What questions do I ask them? What things do I tell them?

What conclusions should they reach? and How can they apply what's been learned?)

2. *Presentation*, in which the new lesson is introduced.
3. *Association*, in which the new lesson is related to previously studied ideas.
4. *Systemization*, in which the rules, principles, and generalizations of the new material is mastered by the learner.
5. *Application*, in which the newly learned material is applied to applicable problems or projects (Herbart, 1894).

Herbart's five successive steps of instruction were endorsed and adopted into the teaching practices of classroom teachers of the day and still serve as guidelines for developmental lessons of today.

Friedrich Froebel (1782–1852). Known for his development of the kindergarten (literally, "the child's garden"), Froebel was a German educator who advocated songs, stories, games, colorful materials, and the manipulation of objects in the educational experiences of young children. Brought to America by German immigrants, the Froebel philosophy fostered organizing the schooling of three- and four-year-old children around individual and group play activities in a secure and pleasant environment where children could develop naturally. Many of Froebel's methods and concepts are found in today's early childhood and kindergarten programs.

The Rise of Universal Education

The U.S. educational system as it is known today began to take form in what has come to be known as the age of the common school movement, which occurred during the period 1830–1865. The term *common school movement* indicated a movement toward state control of schools that were to be attended in common by all students and publicly supported by direct taxation.

The moving forces behind the common school movement were varied. Over a billion square miles of territory were added to the United States between 1830 and 1860. The population boomed from 13 million to over 32 million, with 4 million coming from immigration alone. Growth in industry increased the urban populations, which in turn increased the concentrations of students who needed to be schooled. The working class began to demand common schools that provided the education necessary to equip them with the ability to participate equally in the democracy. Business and industrial leaders also supported the common school movement because they saw it as a way to provide a continuing source of workers who were literate and easier to train. Social groups envisioned common schools as the remedy for social unrest, crime, and the often degrading and uncivil behavior of the illiterate. Educational organizations began to spring up in support of the common school movement and spearheaded the articulation and publicity that were needed to spread public education across the United States (Cremin, 1982).

Funding for elementary schools was slow, but funding for secondary schools came even more slowly. The impetus given by the famous Kalamazoo, Michigan, case of 1874 was significant. The Michigan Supreme Court ruled that the legislature could tax the public for schools at both the elementary and secondary levels. This set a precedent, and by the end of the nineteenth century publicly supported high schools had replaced the academy and become established in every state.

With tax support established, the focus of attention then became the curriculum. At the elementary level, the curriculum was not too complicated. The basic skills of reading, writing, and arithmetic were foremost. The high school, however, with its new emphasis on comprehensive education, made curricular decisions more complex. After Harvard President Charles Eliot chaired the National Education Association's failed Committee of Ten curricular efforts in 1892 (which were aimed almost solely at college preparation), the NEA tried again twenty-five years later with a new committee. That committee was successful in that its recommendations viewed the high school as a much more comprehensive institution, with only one of its educational principles dealing with college preparation. The new NEA committee issued Seven Cardinal Principles of Secondary Education, which identified what the high school curricular objectives should include. The seven cardinal principles, which can still be found in the goals of modern-day social studies programs, include:

1. *Health.* A secondary school should encourage good health habits, give health instruction, and provide physical activities. Good health should be taken into account when schools and communities are planning activities for youth. The general public should be educated on the importance of good health. Teachers should be examples for good health, and schools should furnish good equipment and safe buildings.
2. *Command of fundamental academic skills.* Fundamental processes are writing, reading, oral and written expression, and math. It was decided that these basics should be applied to newer material instead of using the older ways of doing things.
3. *Worthy home membership.* This principle "calls for the development of those qualities that make the individual a worthy member of a family, both contributing to and deriving benefit from that membership" (Raubinger, Rowe, Piper, & West, 1969, p. 108). This principle should be taught through literature, music, social studies, and art. Co-ed schools should promote good relationships between males and females. When trying to instill this principle in students, the future as well as the present should be taken into account.
4. *Vocation.* The objective of this principle is that students get to know themselves and become informed about a variety of careers so that they can choose those careers for which they are best suited. Students should then develop an understanding of the relationship between

their vocation and the community in which they live and work. Those who are successful in a vocation should be the ones to teach the students in either the school or the workplace.

5. *Civic education.* The goal of civic education is to develop an awareness and concern for one's own community. A student should gain knowledge of social organizations and a commitment to civic morality. Diversity and cooperation should be paramount. Democratic organization of the school and classroom, as well as group problem solving, are the methods through which this principle should be taught.
6. *Worthy use of leisure.* The idea behind this principle is that education should give students the skills to enrich their bodies, minds, spirit and personality in their leisure. The school should also provide appropriate recreation. This principle should be taught in all subjects but primarily in music, art, literature, drama, social issues, and science.
7. *Ethical character.* This principle involves instilling in students the notion of personal responsibility and initiative. Appropriate teaching methods and school organization are the primary examples that should be used.

The Twentieth Century and Beyond

The population of the United States has grown at a staggering rate: 50 million in 1880, 76 million in 1900, 106 million in 1920, and 275+ million in 2006. In the nineteenth and twentieth centuries, a significant portion of the population growth was due to immigration. The immigrants brought with them new educational ideas and thinking as well as new and perplexing educational problems. Perhaps even more profound than the population growth was the economic growth of the United States. Railroad expansion brought an end to the American frontier and linked every part of the nation. Global shipping—linked by the railroads, the inland waterways, and, later, the trucking industry—opened vast new markets for U.S. agricultural and manufacturing industries. Such an astounding growth, as one might well imagine, brought with it political and business competition that left deep scars and ignited political reforms, many of which continue to this day. Urbanization intensified, rural schools underwent consolidation, and the general bureaucracy of school administration grew by leaps and bounds.

The Progressive Period.[2] During most of the twentieth century, the term *progressive education* was used to describe ideas and practices that aim to make schools more effective agencies of a democratic society. Although there are numerous differences of style and emphasis among progressive educators, they share the conviction that democracy means active participation by all citizens in social, political and economic decisions that will affect their lives. The education of engaged citizens, according to this perspective, involves two essential elements: (1) *Respect for diversity,* meaning that each individual should be recognized for his or her own abilities, interests, ideas, needs, and cultural identity; and (2) the development of *critical, socially engaged intelligence,* which enables individuals to understand and participate effectively in the affairs of their community in a collaborative effort to achieve a common good. These elements of progressive education have been termed *child-centered* and *social reconstructionist* approaches, and while in extreme forms they have sometimes been separated, in the thought of John Dewey and other major theorists they are seen as being necessarily related to each other.

These progressive principles have never been the predominant philosophy in American education. From their inception in the 1830s, state systems of common or public schooling have primarily attempted to achieve cultural uniformity, not diversity, and to educate dutiful, not critical citizens. Furthermore, schooling has been under constant pressure to support the ever-expanding industrial economy by establishing a competitive meritocracy and preparing workers for their vocational roles.

The term *progressive* arose from a period (roughly 1890–1920) during which many Americans took a more careful look at the political and social effects of vast concentrations of corporate power and private wealth. Dewey, in particular, saw that with the decline of local community life and small-scale enterprise, young people were losing valuable opportunities to learn the arts of democratic participation, and he concluded that education would need to make up for this loss. In his Laboratory School at the University of Chicago, where he worked between 1896 and 1904, Dewey tested ideas he shared with leading school reformers such as Francis W. Parker and Ella Flagg Young. Between 1899 and 1916 he circulated his ideas in works such as *The School and Society, The Child and the Curriculum*, *Schools of Tomorrow,* and *Democracy and Education*, and through numerous lectures and articles. During these years other experimental schools were established around the country, and in 1919 the Progressive Education Association was founded, aiming at "reforming the entire school system of America."

Led by Dewey, progressive educators opposed a growing national movement that sought to separate academic education for the few and narrow vocational training for the masses. During the 1920s, when education turned increasingly to "scientific" techniques such as intelligence testing and cost-benefit management, progressive educators insisted on the importance of the emotional, artistic, and creative aspects of human development. After the Depression began, a group of politically oriented progressive educators, led by George Counts, dared schools to "build a new social order" and published a provocative journal called *The Social Frontier* to advance their "reconstructionist" critique of *laissez-faire* capitalism.

At Teachers College, Columbia University, William H. Kilpatrick and other students of Dewey taught the principles of progressive education to thousands of teachers and school leaders, and in the middle part of the century, books such as Dewey's *Experience and Education* (1938), Boyd Bode's *Progressive Education at the Crossroads* (1938), Caroline Pratt's *I Learn from Children* (1948), and Carlton Washburne's *What is Progressive Education?* (1952), among

Many ideas and practices found in today's classroom have their philosophical roots in progressive education.

others, continued to provide a progressive critique of conventional assumptions about teaching, learning and schooling. A major research endeavor, the *eight-year study* demonstrated that students from progressive high schools were capable, adaptable learners and excelled even in the finest universities.

Nevertheless, in the 1950s, during a time of cold-war anxiety and cultural conservatism, progressive education was widely repudiated, and it disintegrated as an identifiable movement. However, in the years since, various groups of educators have rediscovered the ideas of Dewey and his associates and revised them to address the changing needs of schools, students, and society in the late twentieth and early twenty-first century. Open classrooms, schools without walls, cooperative learning, multiage approaches, whole language, the social curriculum, experiential education, and numerous forms of alternative schools all have important philosophical roots in progressive education. John Goodlad's notion of "nongraded" schools (introduced in the late 1950s), Theodore Sizer's network of "essential" schools, Elliott Wigginton's Foxfire project, and Deborah Meier's student-centered Central Park East schools are some well-known examples of progressive reforms in public education. In the 1960s, critics like Paul Goodman and George Dennison took Dewey's ideas in a more radical direction, helping give rise to the free school movement. In more recent years, activist educators in inner cities have advocated greater equity, justice, diversity and other democratic values through the publication *Rethinking Schools* and through the National Coalition of Education Activists.

Today, scholars, educators and activists are rediscovering Dewey's work and exploring its relevance to a *postmodern* age, an age of global capitalism and breathtaking cultural change, and an age in which the ecological health of the planet itself is seriously threatened. We are finding that although Dewey wrote a century ago, his insights into democratic culture and meaningful education suggest hopeful alternatives to the regime of standardization and mechanization that more than ever dominate our schools.

Notes

[1] Adapted from P. Travers & R. Rebore (1990), *Foundations of Education: Becoming A Teacher* (pp. 69–72, 82). Englewood Cliffs, NJ: Prentice Hall.

[2] Adapted from *A Brief Overview of Progressive Education*, The John Dewey Project on Progressive Education, The University of Vermont. Used by permission.

SECTION II

Components of Secondary Social Studies

Social studies should not be confused with social competence or social education. *Social competence* is the ability to engage in group activities both in and out of school. To shop for groceries, ride a bus, and participate in a meeting are all examples of social competence. *Social education* takes place in the school, in the family, in the church, and in other institutions. It is the way in which individuals develop social competence. Although social studies education contributes to both social competence and social education, it is first and foremost an area of the curriculum, just as are English, mathematics, and biology.

The school subject that we call social studies draws upon several of the social sciences for its content. Often, these social science disciplines are referred to as the *core disciplines* of the social studies. In addition to these core disciplines, the Ten Thematic Strands, as well as instructional scope and sequence, foundational skills, and information literacy, are also important components of secondary social studies.

The Core Disciplines

The core disciplines are comprised of geography, history, civics, economics, anthropology, political science, sociology, and psychology (although many high schools are only able to provide courses in geography, civics, economics, and history [both world and American] because of school size, grad-

Figure 2.1 Core Disciplines

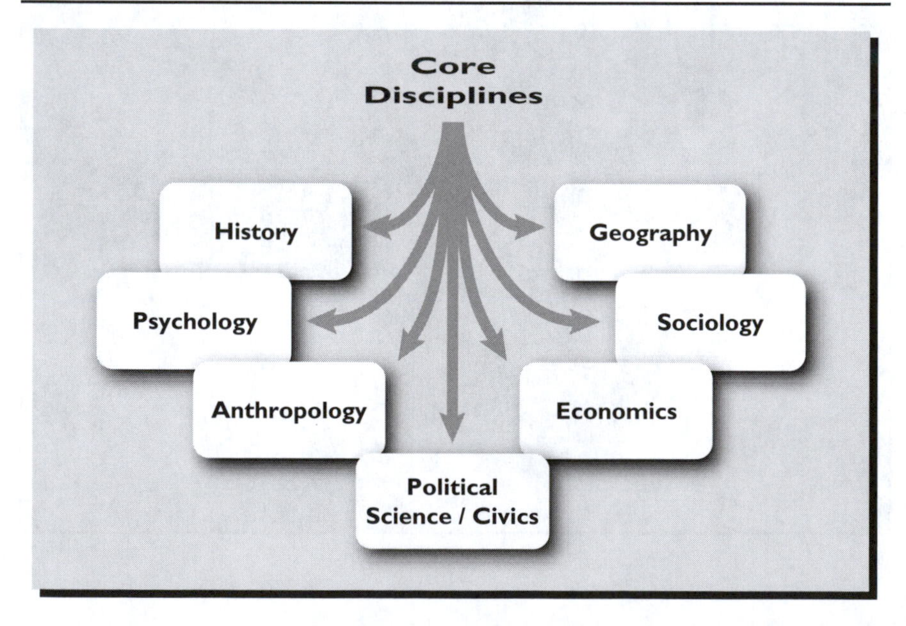

uation requirements, and budget constraints). Social studies in the elementary school may be thought of as a synthesis of these social sciences, because they are blended and integrated together during the teaching of social studies units, themes, and concepts. A thematic unit on the Middle East, for example, would very likely have students investigating the geographical makeup of the region; the historical roots of the Middle East; the economics of the area; the anthropological, cultural hearths of the people; how Middle Eastern countries are governed (who has the power and authority and how it is used); and the societal problems, processes, and institutions of the Middle Eastern countries. In an interdisciplinary approach, this same thematic unit could extend into science, mathematics, language arts, music, and art as well.

Geography[1]

Geography serves as a bridge between the social sciences and the natural sciences and is a major pillar of the social studies curriculum. It explores the spatial variations of the cultural and physical characteristics that make each place on Earth distinctive and unique. The word *geography* was originated by the ancient Greek scholar, Eratosthenes. It is based on two Greek words: *geo,* meaning "the Earth," and *graphy,* meaning "to write." The word geography, then, means literally to write about the Earth.

Geographers ask and seek answers to two simple questions: *where* and *why.* Where are people, places, and activities located on the Earth's surface? Why are they located in those particular places? How people interact with their spatial environment is of the essence to a geographer. Physical geography provides information on landforms, water bodies, climate, weather, and plant and animal life. Human or cultural geography provides information on how people interact with their physical and cultural environments. Human geography ranges from ways people live in selected cultures to other aspects of human settlement on Earth, such as historical, demographic, urban, economic, and political interaction.

Geographic information-processing skills can be grouped under five headings:

- *Asking geographic questions.* Geography is distinguished by the kinds of questions it asks—the "where?" and "why there?" aspects of a problem. It is important for students to develop and practice skills in asking such questions themselves.
- *Acquiring geographic information.* These skills range from identifying locations using grid systems, through making observations and acquiring information in the field, to obtaining statistical data.
- *Presenting geographic information.* These skills involve preparation of maps, tables, and graphs, and coherent written or oral presentations.
- *Interpreting geographic information.* Interpreting involves the ability to determine what a particular map, table, or graph says (e.g., describing trends portrayed on a line graph).

- *Developing and testing geographic information.* These are skills in making inferences based on information contained in maps, tables, and graphs.

Geography is concerned with the following fundamental features of the earth:

- *The movements and positions of the earth* (including orbit, revolution, tilt, and rotation)
- *The hemispheres* (including an understanding of latitude and longitude and the Prime Meridian). Globes and maps are the fundamental tools for geographic learning. Understanding the grid system used by humankind to locate specific places on the Earth's surface is of major importance to everyone, and students should be familiar with using this system by the time they have reached the secondary-school level. Students in the secondary school social studies program should understand the essential role of the Earth's hemispheres in determining latitude and longitude.
- *The lithosphere, hydrosphere, atmosphere, and biosphere* (including trophosphere, stratosphere, mesosphere, thermosphere and ionosphere, as well as an understanding of ecology and biomes). Partitioning the study of geography into the four divisions of the lithosphere (land), the hydrosphere (water), the atmosphere (air), and the biosphere (living) is often very effective. Collaborative groups of students can focus their emphasis on one of these four spheres and, orchestrated by the teacher, prepare reports, charts, graphics, murals, and the like, culminating in a presentation to the other groups.

In 1984, the Association of American Geographers and the National Council for Geographic Education published *Guidelines for Geographic Education,* which identifies the fundamental themes of school geography and develops them explicitly for use by teachers, curriculum developers, and school administrators. The themes are:

1. *Location:* Position on the Earth's Surface
2. *Place:* Natural and Cultural Characteristics
3. *Relationships within Places:* Humans and Environments
4. *Movement:* Humans Interacting on the Earth
5. *Regions:* How They Form and Change

Internet Resources for Teaching Geography

- *The Importance of Geography in the School Curriculum*
  The National Council for Geographic Education offers this pamphlet of information regarding the importance of geography education.
  http://www.ncge.org/publications/resources/importance/

- *Geography Links*
  http://www.geocities.com/dboals.geo/geog.html
- *Geography*
  A collection of geography links from About.com.
  http://geography.about.com/science/geography/
- *Map Lessons: The Route to Improved Geography Skills*
  From Education World, this site features links to more than 20 geography lesson plans.
  http://www.educationworld.com/a_lesson/lesson287.shtml
- *The Nation's Report Card—Geography*
  Includes information on the geography achievement of American students as determined by the National Assessment of Educational Progress.
  http://nces.ed.gov/nationsreportcard/geography/
- *Xpeditions*
  Includes information on the U.S. National Geography Standards, a collection of sites for teaching and learning geography, an online atlas, and other resources. Provided by National Geographic and MarcoPolo.
  http://www.nationalgeographic.com/xpeditions/
- *Population Reference Bureau—Educators Forum*
  Includes tools for teaching about population issues and trends and provides information on teaching standards.
  http://www.prb.org/template.cfm?Section=Educators
- *Census in Schools: Making Sense of Census 2000*
  Includes online interdisciplinary teaching materials for all grade levels, as well as information on how to order additional free teaching materials, ESL and Adult Literacy materials, and more.
  http://www.census.gov/dmd/www/teachers.html
- *Social Science Data Analysis Network*
  From the Population Studies Center at the University of Michigan, this is a university-based organization that creates demographic media, such as user guides, Web sites, and hands-on classroom computer materials that make U.S. census data accessible to educators.
  http://www.ssdan.net/
- *Working with Maps, USGS Learning Web*
  Several activities are presented to assist in teaching the concepts of reading maps. The Teacher Guide explains how the activities are related to locations, places, relationships, movement, and regions. Provides links to other topics on earth science and global changes.
  http://interactive2.usgs.gov/learningweb/teachers/lesson_plans.htm#maps
- *The Geographer's Craft*
  A teaching initiative being pursued in the Department of Geography at the University of Colorado at Boulder to improve the teaching of geo-

graphical techniques at the introductory level.
http://www.Colorado.EDU/geography/gcraft/contents.html

- *National Geographic Map Machine*
  Clickable world map which retrieves country maps, flags, and country information. Also includes selected area maps, political and physical maps, and an interactive Macromedia Shockwave enhanced world map.
  http://www.nationalgeographic.com/resources/ngo/maps/
- *Online Map Creation*
  Lets you draw simple maps interactively. You give the borders of the desired map and specify options, and a map will show up on your Web page.
  http://www.aquarius.geomar.de/omc_intro.html
- *U.S. Gazetteer*
  Browse geographic info, maps and census data for U.S. cities.
  http://www.census.gov/cgi-bin/gazetteer
- *Tiger Mapping Service*
  Provided by the U.S. Census Bureau, this site generates maps from zip codes or city/state info. Census data can also be plotted on maps.
  http://tiger.census.gov
- *National Council for Geographic Education*
  Jacksonville State University
  206A Martin Hall
  Jacksonville, AL 36265-1602
  Phone: (256) 782-5293
  Fax: (256) 782-5336
  Web site: http://www.ncge.org/

History

History might be defined as the description and interpretation of significant past events. In the secondary school, history is a broadly integrative field, recounting and analyzing human aspirations and strivings in at least five spheres of human activity: social, scientific/technological, economic, political, and cultural (i.e., religious/philosophical/aesthetic). Introducing students to history—the history of families, their communities, their state, nation, and various cultures of the world—at once engages them in the aspirations, struggles, accomplishments, and failures of real people, in all these aspects of their lives. Through history:

- Students acquire deeper understandings of society—of different and changing patterns of family structures, of men's and women' roles, of childhood and of children's roles, of various groups in society, and of relationships among all these individuals and groups.
- Students better comprehend the scientific quest to understand the world in which we live and the quest to do better, or more efficiently,

everything from producing food to caring for the ill, to transporting goods, to advancing economic security and the well-being of the group. Understandings of the work people have done, the exchange relationships they have developed with others, and the scientific/technological developments that have propelled change are all central to the study of history and of great interest to students.

- Students begin to understand the political sphere of activity as it has developed in their local community, their state, and their nation. Particularly important are understandings of the core principles and values of American democracy that unite us as a people; of the people and events that have exemplified these principles in local, state, and national history; and of the struggles to bring the rights guaranteed by these principles to all Americans.
- Students come to see that ideas, beliefs, and values have profoundly influenced human actions across time. Religion, philosophy, art, and popular culture have all been central to the aspirations and achievements of all societies and have been a mainspring of historical change from earliest times. Students' explorations of this sphere of human activity, through examination of the literature, sacred writings and oral traditions, drama, art, architecture, music, and dance of a people, bring history to life for children, foster empathy, and deepen their understandings of the human experience.

The Bradley Commission on History in Schools suggested three curricular options for consideration by teachers:

1. *A "here–there–then" approach.* This approach first centers instruction in the student's immediate present and then, each year, reaches out in space and back in time to enlarge the breadth of geographic and historical understandings to distant places and times long ago. From kindergarten onward, this model introduces children to peoples and cultures throughout the world, and to historical times as distant as the earliest human memories contained in myths, legends, and heroic tales, which are part of the cultural heritage of the world.
2. *A modification of the "expanding environments" approach to social studies.* This approach includes, each year, rich studies in history and literature that connect with grade one studies of the family, grade two studies of the neighborhood, grade three studies of the community, grade four studies of the state, grade five studies of the nation, grade six studies of the world, and into the secondary areas of American and world history, but that expand and deepen these studies far beyond their traditional emphasis on the "here and now." This modified model compares family, community, and state today with family life long ago, and with the people and events of earlier times in the historical development of their community and state. This model also com-

pares family and community life in the United States with life in the many cultures from which our increasingly diverse population has come, and with the historical experiences and traditions that are part of those cultures.

3. *A "literature-centered" approach.* This approach focuses instruction each year on compelling selections of appropriate literature from many historical periods and then expands those studies to explore more deeply the historical times they bring to life. This pattern is, essentially, a student's version of the humanities-centered "Great Books" approach to curriculum, with literature used to take students on adventurous and deeply engaging excursions through a variety of historical eras, cultures, and authors' viewpoints.
4. In 1994, the National History Standards Project released national standards in history at the secondary level (for grades 5–12): *National Standards for United States History: Exploring the American Experience* and *National Standards for World History: Exploring Paths to the Present*. These publications are available from the National Center for History in the Schools, UCLA, 10880 Wilshire Boulevard, Suite 761, Los Angeles, CA 90024-4108 (http://www.sscnet.ucla/edu/nchs).

Internet Resources for Teaching History

- *Library of Congress*
  http://www.loc.gov
- *National Archives and Records Administration*
  Historical documents, photographs, search interface for items in Still Picture, Motion Picture, Sound and Video Branches of NARA with ordering information; searchable database of National Archives information resources.
  http://www.nara.gov
- *Perry Castañeda Library Map Collection*
  http://www.lib.utexas.edu/maps/historical/index.html
- *Rare Map Collection at the Hargrett Library*
  http://w2ww.libs.uga.edu/darchive/hargrett/maps/maps/html
- *Interactive Atlas of Culture and History*
  Features over 50 maps dealing with the Antebellum United States and Ancient and Early Medieval Europe. Most have been created with Shockwave, which allows users to follow Roman trade routes, the conquests of Philip and Alexander of Macedon, territorial expansion of the United States through 1853, and the War with Mexico, among other things.
  http://darkwing.uoregon.edu/~atlas/

- *Scope Systems Today-in-History Page*
  Lists celebrity birthdays and historical events for the current date. Also includes a link to two other sites that allow the user to choose any day or any month of any year.
  http://www.scopesys.com/today/
- *History Channel Today-in-History Page*
  http://www.historychannel.com/today
- *Those Were the Days, Today in History*
  Covers the current date and the next; lots of music and sports references
  http://www.440.com/twtd/today.html
- *The National Council for History Education*
  26915 Westwood Road, Suite B-2
  Westlake, Ohio 44145
  Phone: (440) 835-1776
  Fax: (440) 835-1295
  E-mail: nche@nche.net
  Web site: http://www.nche.net/

American History:

- *The Nation's Report Card—U.S. History*
  Includes information on the U.S. history achievement of American students as determined by the National Assessment of Educational Progress.
  http://nces.ed.gov/nationsreportcard/ushistory/
- *America's Library (Library of Congress)*
  A small sample of what you can find at this site: Discover what Abraham Lincoln had in his pockets on the night he was assassinated, jump back into the past to find more about the settlers who landed on Plymouth Rock, or learn how the oud, zurna, and marimba influenced today's modern musical instruments. Focuses on revealing history in a fun and interesting way, using primary source materials such as letters, diaries, photographs, and more.
  http://www.americaslibrary.gov/
- *American Cultural History: The Twentieth Century*
  Contains comprehensive discussions of life in each decade of the twentieth century in the United States. Includes information on people and personalities, fashions and fads, events, music, education, and statistics (e.g., salary, population, prices). Links are provided to related Web resources.
  http://kclibrary/nhmccd.edu/decades.html
- *New American Studies Web*
  Includes Economy and Politics, Race and Ethnicity, Gender and Sexuality, Social Science, Current Events and Legal Studies, and more.
  http://www.georgetown.edu/crossroads/asw/
- *Crossroads: A K–16 American History Curriculum*
  Composed of 36 elementary, middle, and high school units chronolog-

ically organized into 12 historical periods, as well as course syllabi for pre-service social studies educators on the subjects of American history and history education.
http://eduref.org/Virtual/Lessons/crossroads/

- *Douglass: Archives of American Public Address*
A collection of important American speeches searchable by date, title, speaker, and by "controversy or movement." Also contains links to related Web resources.
http://douglassarchives.org/
- *Library of Congress American Memory Project*
Over 70 collections of digitized documents, photographs, recorded sound, moving pictures, and text from the Library's Americana collections. There is also a Learning Page to help educators and students using the collection in the classroom.
http://memory.loc.gov/ammem/index.html
- *ushistory.org*
From the Independence Hall in Philadelphia, this site features early American history. Resources include the Declaration of Independence, Thomas Paine, the Revolutionary War, and more.
http://www.ushistory.org/
- *Making of America*
". . . a digital library of primary sources in American social history from the antebellum period through reconstruction. The collection is particularly strong in the subject areas of education, psychology, American history, sociology, religion, and science and technology."
http://moa.umdl.umich.edu/
- *Ben's Guide to U.S. Government for Kids*
Provides learning tools for K–12 students, parents, and teachers about how U.S. government works. Provided by Superintendent of Documents, U.S. Government Printing Office (GPO).
http://bensguide.gpo.gov/
- *Educational Links—U.S. House of Representatives*
Includes the full text of the U.S. Constitution, amendments, and articles.
http://www.house.gov/house/Educate.shtml
- *From Revolution to Reconstruction . . . and What Happened Afterwards*
Information on U.S. presidents, including speeches, biographies, and links to Web sites dedicated to American presidents
http://odur.let.rug.nl/~usa/P/
- *Teacher & Student Resources at the INS*
Provides resources on the history of immigration to the United States. Find out about famous symbols of immigration to America, including the Statue of Liberty and Ellis Island. Learn more about genealogy to help you discover information about your own immigrant background.
http://uscis.gov/graphics/aboutus/history/teacher/index.htm

- *Documenting the American South*
  A collection of sources on Southern history, literature and culture from the colonial period through the first decades of the twentieth century. Includes a library of Southern literature, slave narratives, and community perspectives.
  http://docsouth.unc.edu/
- *American Journeys*
  ". . . contains more than 18,000 pages of eyewitness accounts of North American exploration, from the sagas of Vikings in Canada in AD 1000 to the diaries of mountain men in the Rockies 800 years later." A collaborative project of the Wisconsin Historical Society and National History Day.
  http://www.americanjourneys.org/
- *Archiving Early America*
  Primary source material from eighteenth-century America.
  http://www.earlyamerica.com/
- *At Home in the Heartland Online*
  In-depth materials on family life in Illinois from 1700 to the present.
  http://museum.state.il.us/exhibits/athome/welcome.htm
- *African-American Women: On-line Archival Collections*
  Presents the letters and memoirs of three African-American women in the nineteenth century.
  http://scriptorium.lib.duke.edu/collections/african-american-women.html
- *Exploring the West from Monticello*
  An online collection of maps documenting the westward exploration of America.
  http://www.lib.virginia.edu/exhibits/lewis_clark/home.html
- *PBS Online: Lewis and Clark*
  Information on the expedition of Lewis and Clark and classroom resources for teachers.
  http://www.pbs.org/lewisandclark/index.html
- *The New Deal Network*
  Online resources on FDR, the Great Depression, and New Deal programs.
  http://newdeal.feri.org/
- *The Papers of George Washington*
  Materials on George Washington's life and a selection of his papers.
  http://www.gwpapers.virginia.edu
- *Africans in America*
  "America's journey through slavery is presented in four parts. For each era, you'll find a historical Narrative, a Resource Bank of images, documents, stories, biographies, and commentaries, and a Teacher's

Guide for using the content of the Web site and television series in U.S. history courses."
http://www.pbs.org/wgbh/aia/home.html

Economics

Economics, one of the newer social sciences, studies the production, distribution, exchange, and consumption of goods and services that people need or want. In a real sense, it is the study of how people use a finite number of resources to satisfy an infinite number of wants. Economists study the ways in which individuals use material resources, how *producers* and *consumers* compare, and how *goods* and *services* compare.

Scarcity, specialization, interdependence, market, and public policy were identified by Skeel (1995) as important, basic concepts in economics. *Scarcity* means that a choice must be made in the allocation of material resource—there is not enough of a particular resource, whether money, time, or gas, to put it to all the uses that people want, and they therefore must make choices. *Specialization* refers to making the choice of completing only one type of task. Sandy does only the cooking while Ross does the cleaning, or one factory worker drills the holes in the steel while another installs the bolts. A *market* means there is need for goods or services that have been produced or provided. *Interdependence* demonstrates that the individual cannot produce all the things needed and is dependent on others for goods and services. *Public policy* is the decision-making process that determines what will or will not be produced.

In social studies, economics helps pupils understand how different societies allocate their resources, why different societies use their resources in different ways, and what factors contribute to such decisions. One economics concept that students grasp rather quickly is scarcity because, at some point, they have experienced not having something they needed or wanted. The concept of scarcity necessitates decision making on the part of the student, and this is easy to convert to an understanding of how societies also must make decisions based on scarcity.

Some ways to pursue economic education include (1) examining ways people depend on one another, (2) comparing work roles, (3) studying different types of advertising, (4) comparing wages, (5) role-playing negotiations, (6) using newspapers, (7) studying the concept of seasonal employment, (8) studying government regulations, (9) familiarizing students with local businesses, (10) studying personal and family budgeting, and (11) participating in simulation games (Monopoly and the stock market simulation, for example).

Internet Resources for Teaching Economics

- *World Bank Teachers and Students Home Page (Youthink!)*
  Contains educational materials dealing with international economic conditions and other issues impacting the economic development of

nations such as population, climate change, and disease; includes subscription instructions for the Youthink! newsletter
http://youthink.worldbank.org/

- *Voluntary National Content Standards in Economics*
  Produced by the National Council on Economic Education, EconomicsAmerica.
  http://www.ncee.net.ea/program.php?pid=19
- *EcEdWeb: Economic Ed Website*
  Provides support for learning economics in all forms and at all levels. For lesson suggestions, check out the Curricular Materials section or examine the idea page on how to teach economics using the Internet.
  http://ecedweb.unomaha.edu/
- *EconEdLink*
  Contains links to economics resources and data as well as online lesson plans and activities for exploring the connections between economics and real-world issues.
  http://www.econedlink.org/
- *Journal of Economic Education*
  ". . . offers original articles on innovations in and evaluations of teaching techniques, materials, and programs in economics. Tailored to the needs of instructors of introductory through graduate-level economics, covering content and pedagogy in a variety of mediums." Online articles (1998–present) are available in pdf format.
  http://www.indiana.edu/~econed/index.html
- *Economic Education Publications and Resources*
  From the Federal Reserve Bank of Chicago, this site features publications for the general public and high school/college students on topics such as understanding interest rates, international trade, electronic money, international monetary exchange rates, and more; several resources include classroom-ready lesson plans.
  http://chicagofed.org/education_resources/index.cfm
- *Young Investor Web Site*
  Designed to teach students about banks, money, and investing.
  http://www.younginvestor.com
- *The Mint*
  This integrated Web site, designed for middle school and high school students, their teachers and parents, includes information on saving and investing, starting your own business, government spending, the financial rewards of continuing education, spending habits and the economy, a dictionary of related vocabulary, and other resources to help students better understand finance and economics.
  http://www.themint.org/

- *STAT-USA/Internet*
  Provides access to thousands of data files, more than 700 of them updated daily. Includes information about current economic conditions, economic indicators, employment, foreign trade, monetary matters and more in 20 general subject areas. Source: gopher/off-campus services/points of interest.
  http://www.stat-usa.gov
- *Resources for Economists on the Internet*
  Includes links to more than 700 economics resources.
  http://www.rfe.org
- *Wall Street Research Net*
  Provides users with a large company database and economic research.
  http://www.wsrn.com/
- *New York Stock Exchange (NYSE)*
  Designed as an educational tool for investors, students and teachers, this site provides links to a rich diversity of information.
  http://www.nyse.com/
- *American Stock Exchange*
  http://www.amex.com/
- *Yahoo's daily stock market reports/updates*
  http://finance.yahoo.com/
- *Better Business Bureau*
  Provides information on more than 2.5 million organizations (useful for young investors).
  http://www.bbb.org/
- *What is a Market Economy?*
  An electronic version of a publication by Michael Watts, originally produced in print by the Bureau of Information of the U.S. Information Agency.
  http://usinfo.org/trade/market/index.htm
- *EconData*
  Provides links to socioeconomic data sources and pointers to online data collections to help users locate regional economic data.
  http://www.econdata.net
- *Economic Glossarama*
  Contains a glossary of more than 1000 economic terms and concepts.
  http://www.amosweb.com/gls/

Organizations

- *National Council on Economic Education*
  1140 Avenue of the Americas
  New York, NY 10036
  Phone: (212) 730-7007

Fax: (212) 730-1793
E-mail: info@ncee.net
Web site: http://www.ncee.net/

- *National Institute for Consumer Education*
559 Gary M. Owen Building
300 W. Michigan Avenue
Eastern Michigan University
Ypsilanti, MI 48197
Phone: (734) 487-2292
Fax: (734) 487-7153
E-mail: NICE@emuvax.emich.edu
Web site: http://www.nice.emich.edu/
- *National Endowment for Financial Education*
5299 DTC Boulevard, Suite 1300
Englewood, CO 80111-3334
Phone: (303) 741-6333
Web site: http://www.nefe.org/
- *The Jump$tart Coalition for Personal Financial Literacy*
919 18th Street, N.W.
Suite 300
Washington, DC 20006
Phone: (888) 45-EDUCATE
Fax: (202) 223-0321
E-mail: info@jumpstartcoalition.org
Web site: http://www.jumpstart.org/

Anthropology

Anthropology is often seen as the unifying social science because it is a study of humans, their cultures, how they adapt to their environments, and their growth toward civilization. It is concerned with such things as the development of languages, religions, art, and physical and mental traits. Every society has a culture made up of its beliefs, values, and traditions. Culture is socially learned. People of different cultures have the same psychological and physiological needs but meet their needs differently, based on their culture.

Anthropologists study the ways in which people live in various and diverse cultures, human beings within cultures, and how people interact with culture. They seek knowledge about the customs, laws, traditions, and beliefs of people within a culture and look at physical characteristics, such as race. Examining the religions of people often leads anthropologists to what may be termed humankind's "cultural hearths." Knowledge of both universal and particular traits of the diverse peoples of the world is provided by anthropologists who get most of their information through field studies, where they actually live for prolonged periods within a culture, and from archeological excavations.

Students can develop an appreciation for anthropology and for the work of the anthropologist through skits and simulations in which they practice fieldwork within a simulated culture. Also, simulated digs can be staged with items from our culture buried (planted) by one cooperative group of pupils and excavated by another cooperative group.

Internet Resources for Anthropology

- *ASOR Outreach Education*
  Archaeology resources for teachers and students, including an Ask an Archaeologist section. Provided by the American Schools of Oriental Research.
  http://www.asor.org/outreach/default.htm
- *Anthropology Resources on the Internet*
  A collection of sites from the American Anthropological Association.
  http://www.aaanet.org/resinet.htm
- *Other Anthropology Web Site Links*
  http://eclectic.ss.uci.edu/~drwhite/anthro.htm (a good "doorway" to other sites)
  http://www.lib.panam.edu/research/websites/anthropology.asp (simple and easy to navigate)
- *ArchNet WWW Virtual Library of Archaeology*
  Includes links to information on specific regions and subject areas, academic departments, museums, and other related resources.
  http://archnet.asu.edu/
- *Texas A&M Online Anthropology Communities*
  Provides a list of links for subscribing to many discussion groups on numerous topics.
  http://anthropology/tamu.edu/discussions.htm
- *ANTHRO-L*
  A general anthropology mailing list.
  http://danny.oz/au/communities/anthro-l/
- *American Anthropological Association*
  4350 North Fairfax Drive, Suite 640
  Arlington, VA 22203-1620
  Phone: (703) 528-1902
  Fax: (703) 528-3546
  Web site: http://www.aaanet.org/
- *Society for American Archaeology*
  900 Second Street NE, #12
  Washington, DC 20002-3557
  Phone: (202) 789-8200
  Fax: (202) 789-0284

E-mail: headquarters@saa.org
Web site: http://www.saa.org/

Political Science and Civics

Political science is the study of government: the political processes, political behavior, political decision making, and the tasks, processes, and services of government. In essence, political science is the study of power and authority. Perhaps one of the more interesting and intriguing aspects of political science is the study of the ways in which people interact with power and authority. All societies have developed ways of keeping social order; all have a structure of power and authority. The governmental enforcers of the rules have great power over individuals in the society.

Central governments expect and demand loyalty when they are threatened by hostile forces. Political socialization (civics) is a way of inducting the young into the political life of the society. While basic political orientation is well established in early years when growing up in a society, and in primary grades children learn that when people live together in groups (e.g., the classroom, the community, the city) they need rules, in upper grades and secondary school children can explore *why* nations and governments form alliances. Often, this can be configured with current events studies.

According to Thomas Jefferson, preparation for the office of citizen is the crucial purpose of American education. The vitality of American constitutional democracy depends on competent citizens. Full literacy for the twenty-first century demands a challenging education with adequate attention to all academic disciplines. Effective social studies education reinforces the democratic principles and ideals of citizenship. A solid base of social studies knowledge and skills develops civic competence by focusing on rights, responsibilities, and respect.

Major concepts to be considered in political science and civics would include political systems, power, authority, political behavior, public policies, and political socialization.

Internet Resources for Political Science and Civics

- *Justice Learning*
  An innovative, issue-based approach for engaging high school students in informed political discourse, using audio from the *Justice Talking* radio show and articles from *The New York Times* to teach about reasoned debate and the often-conflicting values inherent in our democracy.
  http://www.justicelearning.org/teachingmaterials.asp
- *The Civic Mission of Schools*
  Summarizes the evidence in favor of civic education in K–12 schools; analyzes trends in political and civic engagement; identifies promising approaches to civic education; and offers recommendations to educa-

tors, policy makers, funders, researchers, and others. Written and endorsed by a distinguished and diverse group of more than 50 scholars and practitioners.
http://www.civicmissionofschools.org/

- *Justice Learning: Civic Education in the Real World*
  A collaboration of NPR's *Justice Talking* and *The New York Times* Learning Network, this is an innovative, issue-based approach for engaging high school students in informed political discourse.
  http://www.justicelearning.org

- *The Role of Civic Education*
  Defines civic education, its essential components, where and how it takes place, the need to improve, and the relationship between civic education and character education.
  http://www.civiced.org/articles_role.html

- *Civic Education: Recent History, Current Status, and the Future*
  Presented at the American Bar Association Symposium, "Public Perception and Understanding of the Justice System," Washington, DC, February 25–26, 1999, by Charles N. Quigley, executive director of the Center for Civic Education.
  http://www.civiced.org/papers_quigley99.html

- *The Nation's Report Card—Civics*
  The National Assessment of Educational Progress (NAEP) regularly reports to the public on the educational progress of students in grades 4, 8, and 12. This site provides a link to the 1998 Civics results.
  http://nces.ed.gov/nationsreportcard/civics/

- *National Standards for Civics and Government*
  Voluntary "National Standards for Civics and Government" for students in kindergarten through twelfth grade developed by the Center for Civic Education. More than three thousand teachers, scholars, parents, elected officials, and representatives of business and industry contributed to the Standards' development.
  http://www.civiced.org/stds.html

- *IEA Civic Education Study*
  "Researchers surveyed nearly 90,000 14-year-old students in 28 countries during the second phase of the International Association for the Evaluation of Educational Achievement's Civic Education Study." A link is provided to the pdf version of the first results in the Publications and Reports IEA section.
  http://www2.hu-berlin.de/empir_bf/iea._e.html

- *CIVNET: International Resource for Civic Education and Civic Society*
  Includes a bi-monthly journal on civic society and resources for civic education practitioners.
  http://civnet.org/

- *Civics Online*
  "A collaborative, online project providing a rich array of primary sources, professional development tools, and interactive activities to help in the teaching of civics."
  http://civics-online.org/
- *Facing History and Ourselves*
  National educational organization devoted to engaging students of diverse backgrounds in civic education.
  http://www.facinghistory.org/facing/fhao2.nsf
- *ABA Division for Public Education—K–12 Youth Education*
  "The schools program of the ABA Division for Public Education actively promotes partnerships among educators, legal professionals and others interested in educating children about the law and citizenship."
  http://www.abanet.org/publiced/youth/home.html
- *The Death Penalty Curricula for High School*
  Individual state laws determine whether and how the death penalty is used in each state. Students can explore history, law, state-by-state data, arguments for and against capital punishment, and actual courtroom cases. This site includes teacher overviews and lesson plans for high school civics.
  Teacher Edition: http://teacher.deathpenaltyinfo.msu.edu/
  Student Edition: http://deathpenaltyinfo.msu.edu/
- *CongressLink*
  Provides resources for teachers and students of history, politics, civics, and related subjects. This site promotes student-centered and inquiry-based approaches to learning. Designed for students in the upper elementary grades through college.
  http://www.congresslink.org/
- *Democratic National Committee*
  http://www.democrats.org/index.html
- *Republican National Committee*
  http://www.rnc.org/
- *Vote Smart Web*
  Project Vote Smart, a nonprofit organization, makes factual information about politicians available for free. Their database is available in conjunction with other sources of political information found on the Internet and is researcher assisted via an 800 number.
  http://www.vote-smart.org/
- *H-TeachPol*
  An online community devoted to the discussion of issues regarding political science teaching in post-secondary settings, co-sponsored by the American Political Science Association.
  http://www.h-net.org/~teachpol/

Organizations

- *American Political Science Association*
  The major professional society for individuals engaged in the study of politics and government.
  1527 New Hampshire Avenue NW
  Washington, DC 20036
  Phone: (202) 483-2512
  Web site: http://www.apsanet.org/
- *Center for Civic Education*
  5146 Douglas Fir Rd.
  Calabasas, CA, 91302-1467
  Phone: (818) 591-9321
  Fax: (818) 591-9330
  E-mail: cce@civiced.org
  Web site: http://www.civiced.org/
- *Youth Leadership Initiative*
  ". . . a national citizenship education and engagement program designed to involve students in the American electoral and policy-making process."
  2400 Old Ivy Road
  P. O. Box 400806
  Charlottesville, VA 22904
  Toll-free phone: 1 (866) 514-8389
  Phone: (434) 243-8468
  Fax: (434) 243-8467
  Web site: http://www.youthleadership.net
- *Close Up Foundation*
  44 Canal Center Plaza
  Alexandria, VA 22314-1592
  Toll-free phone: 1 (800) CLOSE UP (256-7387)
  TTY: 800-336-2167
  Web site: http://www.closeup.org/
- *Constitutional Rights Foundation*
  601 South Kingsley Drive
  Los Angeles, CA 90005
  Phone: (213) 487-5590
  Fax: (213) 386-0459
  Web site: http://www.crf-usa.org/

Sociology

Sociology is the study of social institutions, processes, and problems. Sociologists study ways in which people interact with the general society. They examine the social system, particularly the institutions of the social order and the grouping instinct whereby people participate in family groups, church groups, social groups, and the like. Sociologists look at the structure of society in its groups, subgroups, social classes, and institutions.

Some key concepts to be developed in sociology include socialization, society, group, role, social control, social class, status, and institution. Major sociological generalizations for the secondary school might include (1) looking at the family as the basic social unit, (2) examining evidence that every society has had social classes, (3) finding that every society develops a system of roles and values, (4) discovering that all societies develop a system of social control, and (5) understanding that a person's social environment has a profound effect on his or her personal growth and development. Investigating social problems existing in the local community, as well as in the city, state, and global communities, is well within the purview of secondary social studies students. Such sociological investigations can often involve collaborative group work as well as extensive use of technological resources.

Internet Resources for Teaching Sociology

- *Teaching Sociology*
  A quarterly publication of the American Sociological Association, located at the Department of Sociology and Anthropology at Le Moyne College, the Jesuit College of Central New York. This page also includes a link to the *Teaching Sociology Discussion Group.*
  http://www.lemoyne.edu/ts/tscyber.html
- *SOSIG: Social Science Information Gateway—Sociology*
  Links to everything sociological, including journals, educational materials, governmental bodies, databases, mailing lists/discussion groups, organizations/societies, papers/reports/articles, and more.
  http://www.sosig.ac.uk/sociology/
- *Allyn & Bacon's Sociology Links*
  A collection of resources provided by the publisher on a range of topics including theory, race inequality, socialization, deviance, and more.
  http://www.abacon.com/sociology/soclinks/index.html
- *WWW Virtual Library: Sociology Discussions*
  Indexes to mailing lists, archived listservs, and usenet newsgroups.
  http://socserv2.mcmaster.ca/w3bvirtsoclib/discuss.htm
- *American Sociological Association*
  1307 New York Avenue, NW, Suite 700
  Washington, DC 20005
  Phone: (202) 383-9005
  Fax: (202) 638-0882
  TDD: (202) 872-0486
  E-mail: about@asanet.org
  Web site: http://www.asanet.org/

Psychology

The social science that engages in the study of the behavior of individuals is psychology. It concerns the study of the self. Psychologists study the ways in which people interact with themselves via their personalities, identities, and self-concepts. Psychologists investigate the emotional and behavioral characteristics of an individual, a group, or an activity. Controlling feelings, attitude development, a wholesome self-concept, and individual needs are some of the ways that psychology pervades all areas of the instructional program. Motives, interests, personality, sensory learning, self-expression, and self-actualization are key concepts to be developed.

Internet Resources for Teaching Psychology

- *TOPSS: Teachers of Psychology in Secondary Schools*
  From the American Psychological Association, this site includes Standards for the Teaching of High School Psychology, Curriculum Resources, Teacher Resources and Services, Student Resources and Services, and more.
  http://www.apa.org/ed/topss/
- *Contemporary Philosophy of Mind: An Annotated Bibliography*
  A bibliography of recent work in the philosophy of mind, philosophy of cognitive science, and philosophy of artificial intelligence. It consists of 2395 entries and is divided into five parts, each of which is further divided by topic and subtopic.
  http://www.u.arizona.edu/~chalmers/biblio.html
- *Current Topics in Psychology*
  Created by clinical psychologist Michael Fenichel, this hotlist links to general reference and topic-specific articles, Web sites and research tools.
  http://www.fenichel.com/Current.shtml
- *Online Psych*
  Contains public information on a variety of psychological conditions, including more than 250 Internet links in 25 different areas related to mental health information and services on a wide variety of topics.
  http://www.onlinepsych.com/home.html
- *School Psychology Resources Online*
  This hotlist links to sites of interest to the school psychology community.
  http://www.schoolpsychology.net/
- *American Psychological Association*
  750 First Street, NE
  Washington, DC 20002
  Phone: 202/336-5500
  Web site: http://www.apa.org/

Discussion Groups

- *PSYCOLOQUY*
  A refereed electronic journal of peer discussion.
  http://www.princeton.edu/~harnad/psyc.html
- *PSYCH-NEWS (Teaching High School Psychology discussion)*
  Offers descriptions of teaching activities, updates on research in psychology, lists of books, articles, videos and films, and news about conferences high school teachers may find useful. Also provides a forum for teachers to raise questions and make suggestions.
  http://www.lsoft.com/scripts/
  wl.exe?SL2=1043&R=3391&N=PSYCH-NEWS@LISTSERV.UH.EDU
- *PSYCHE*
  The site of an electronic journal which provides information on how to subscribe, post, and use databases in all their related discussion groups.
  http://psyche.cs.monash.edu/au/psychefaq.html
- *PsychNews International*
  An independent electronic Internet-based publication on issues related to the mental health profession. This Web site features subscription instructions for many psychology-related discussions groups/listservs.
  http://userpage.fu-berlin.de/~expert/psychnews/1_4/pni4_1c.htm

Instructional Concerns

The social studies are crucial if we expect the young people of this nation to become active citizens responsible for maintaining the democratic values on which this nation was established. Basic skills of reading, writing, and computing are necessary but not sufficient to participate or even survive in a world that demands independent and cooperative problem solving to address complex social, economic, ethical, and personal concerns. Knowledge, skills, and attitudes necessary for informed and thoughtful participation in society require a systematically developed program focusing on concepts from history, geography, and the social sciences.

Teacher education in social studies has the task of ensuring that teachers have sufficient content knowledge in history, geography, and the other social sciences; knowledge about and skill in different teaching techniques; an ability to locate, evaluate, and use appropriate resources to supplement the text; sufficient knowledge regarding the characteristics and abilities of the student population; and an enthusiasm for teaching social studies that comes from an understanding of the importance of social studies in the K–12 years and an appreciation for and understanding of social studies content.

Social studies often synthesizes the core disciplines by blending, integrating, and orchestrating them during the teaching of social studies units, themes, and concepts, particularly in the subjects of American history, world history, geography, economics, and political science/civics. Secondary teachers in these subjects must probe deeply into the content, using not only textual resources, but the full compliment of literature, technology, and collaborative resources available to today's high school teachers.

Scope and Sequence

Scope represents the breadth, depth, and range of the social studies program; *sequence* represents its order and progression. These criteria are the basic requirements that should be addressed by any social studies scope-and-sequence design, and they take into account three dimensions: (1) scholarship in history, the social sciences, and related fields; (2) the needs of our society in its local, national, and global settings; and (3) the needs, interests, and developmental characteristics of students. The NCSS Ad Hoc Committee on Scope and Sequence developed the following criteria.[2]

A social studies scope and sequence should:

- state the purpose and rationale of the program;
- be internally consistent with its stated purposes and rationale;
- designate content at every grade level, K–12;
- recognize that learning is cumulative;
- reflect a balance of local, national, and global content;
- reflect a balance of past, present, and future content;
- provide for students' understanding of the structure and function of social, economic, and political institutions;
- emphasize concepts and generalizations from history and the social sciences;
- promote the integration of skills and knowledge;
- promote the integration of content across subject areas;
- promote the use of a variety of teaching methods and instructional materials;
- foster active learning and social interaction;
- reflect a clear commitment to democratic beliefs and values;
- reflect a global perspective;
- foster the knowledge and appreciation of cultural heritage;
- foster the knowledge and the appreciation of diversity;
- foster the building of self-esteem;
- be consistent with current research pertaining to how children learn;
- be consistent with current scholarship in the disciplines;
- incorporate thinking skills and interpersonal skills at all levels;

- stress the identification, understanding, and solution of local, national, and global problems;
- provide many opportunities for students to learn and practice the basic skills of participation from observation to advocacy;
- promote the transfer of knowledge and skills to life; and
- have the potential to challenge and excite students.

Content Standards[3]

As mentioned earlier, the framework for social studies in almost every state rests on the foundation of four core disciplines, or strands, from the social sciences: *geography*, *civics*, *economics*, and *history*. Each of these disciplines offers a distinct perspective for examining the world. Other social sciences, such as anthropology and sociology, are incorporated within these strands. In the *content standards*, each of the strand titles names a traditional field of scholarly study, with a phrase explaining the underlying themes. For each strand, a focus paragraph explains the discipline's importance to the overall education of the students. A standard statement then gives a general description of what students should know and be able to do as a result of the study of that strand. Following each standard, specific benchmarks are listed for grades K–4, 5–8, and 9–12.

For organizational purposes, these benchmarks are categorized according to appropriate content standards. Intended as a blueprint for curricular decisions in social studies, the rigorous framework promotes local flexibility in curricular design, course sequence, assessment methods, and instructional strategies. The social studies curriculum should expand students' thinking across the boundaries of separate academic subjects. A reasonable balance between breadth of content and depth of inquiry must be achieved. Through mastery of the key concepts and process skills in these content standards, students will become accomplished problem solvers and informed decision makers. They will be able to assume their places in the economic workforce as effective producers and consumers, and civic competence will have been achieved.

For more information on correlating content standards with benchmarks and grade-level expectations, see Section V.

The Ten Thematic Strands of the Standards for Social Studies

Not to be confused with the content standards and the four core disciplines, the *thematic strands* are key social studies concepts developed and presented by the National Council for the Social Studies. The thematic strands form the basis for the content standards.

The ten themes that form the framework of the social studies standards are:

Culture

The study of culture prepares students to answer questions such as: What are the common characteristics of different cultures? How do belief systems, such as religion or political ideals, influence other parts of the culture? How does the culture change to accommodate different ideas and beliefs? What does language tell us about the culture? In schools, this theme typically appears in units and courses dealing with geography, history, sociology, and anthropology, as well as multicultural topics across the curriculum.

Students in high school can understand and use complex cultural concepts such as adaptation, assimilation, acculturation, diffusion, and dissonance drawn from anthropology, sociology, and other disciplines to explain how culture and cultural systems function.

Time, Continuity, and Change

Human beings seek to understand their historical roots and to locate themselves in time. Knowing how to read and reconstruct the past allows one to develop an historical perspective and to answer questions such as: Who am I? What happened in the past? How am I connected to those in the past? How has the world changed and how might it change in the future? Why does our personal sense of relatedness to the past change? This theme typically appears in courses in history and others that draw upon historical knowledge and habits.

High school students engage in more sophisticated analysis and reconstruction of the past, examining its relationship to the present and extrapolating into the future. They integrate individual stories about people, events, and situations to form a more holistic conception, in which continuity and change are linked in time and across cultures. Students also learn to draw on their knowledge of history to make informed choices and decisions in the present.

People, Places, and Environments

The study of people, places, and human environment interactions assists students as they create their spatial views and geographic perspectives of the world beyond their personal locations. Students need the knowledge, skills, and understanding to answer questions such as: Where are things located? Why are they located where they are? What do we mean by "region"? How do landforms change? What implications do these changes have for people? In schools, this theme typically appears in units and courses dealing with area studies and geography.

Students in high school are able to apply geographic understanding across a broad range of fields, including the fine arts, sciences, and humanities. Geographic concepts become central to learners' comprehension of global connections as they expand their knowledge of diverse cultures, both historical and contemporary. The importance of core geographic themes to public policy is recognized and should be explored as students address issues of domestic and international significance.

Individual Development and Identity

Personal identity is shaped by one's culture, by groups, and by institutional influences. Students should consider such questions as: How do people learn? Why do people behave as they do? What influences how people learn, perceive, and grow? How do people meet their basic needs in a variety of contexts? How do individuals develop from youth to adulthood? In schools, this theme typically appears in units and courses dealing with psychology and anthropology.

At the high school level, students need to encounter multiple opportunities to examine contemporary patterns of human behavior, using methods from the behavioral sciences to apply core concepts drawn from psychology, social psychology, sociology, and anthropology as they apply to individuals, societies, and cultures.

Individuals, Groups, and Institutions

Institutions such as schools, churches, families, government agencies, and the courts play an integral role in people's lives. It is important that students learn how institutions are formed, what controls and influences them, how they influence individuals and culture, and how they are maintained or changed. Students may address questions such as: What is the role of institutions in this and other societies? How am I influenced by institutions? How do institutions change? What is my role in institutional change? In schools this theme typically appears in units and courses dealing with sociology, anthropology, psychology, political science, and history.

High school students must understand the paradigms and traditions that undergird social and political institutions. They should be provided opportunities to examine, use, and add to the body of knowledge related to the behavioral sciences and social theory as it relates to the ways people and groups organize themselves around common needs, beliefs, and interests.

Power, Authority, and Governance

Understanding the historical development of structures of power, authority, and governance and their evolving functions in contemporary U.S. society and other parts of the world is essential for developing civic competence. In exploring this theme, students confront questions such as: What is power? What forms does it take? Who holds it? How is it gained, used, and justified? What is legitimate authority? How are governments created, structured, maintained, and changed? How can individual rights be protected within the context of majority rule? In schools, this theme typically appears in units and courses dealing with government, politics, political science, history, law, and other social sciences.

High school students develop their abilities in the use of abstract principles. They study the various systems that have been developed over the centuries to allocate and employ power and authority in the governing process. At every level, learners should have opportunities to apply their knowledge and skills to and participate in the workings of the various levels of power, authority, and governance.

Production, Distribution, and Consumption

Because people have wants that often exceed the resources available to them, a variety of ways have evolved to answer such questions as: What is to be produced? How is production to be organized? How are goods and services to be distributed? What is the most effective allocation of the factors of production (land, labor, capital, and management)? In schools, this theme typically appears in units and courses dealing with economic concepts and issues.

High school students develop economic perspectives and deeper understanding of key economic concepts and processes through systematic study of a range of economic and sociopolitical systems, with particular emphasis on the examination of domestic and global economic policy options related to matters such as health care, resource use, unemployment, and trade.

Science, Technology, and Society

Modern life as we know it would be impossible without technology and the science that supports it. But technology brings with it many questions: Is new technology always better than old? What can we learn from the past about how new technologies result in broader social change, some of which is unanticipated? How can we cope with the ever-increasing pace of change? How can we manage technology so that the greatest number of people benefit from it? How can we preserve our fundamental values and beliefs in the midst of technological change? This theme draws upon the natural and physical sciences, social sciences, and the humanities, and it appears in a variety of social studies courses, including history, geography, economics, civics, and government.

High school students will need to think more deeply about how we can manage technology so that we control it rather than the other way around. There should be opportunities to confront such issues as the consequences of using robots to produce goods, the protection of privacy in the age of computers and electronic surveillance, and the opportunities and challenges of genetic engineering, test-tube life, and medical technology with all their implications for longevity and quality of life and religious beliefs.

Global Connections

The realities of global interdependence require understanding the increasingly important and diverse global connections among world societies and the frequent tension between national interests and global priorities. Students will need to be able to address such international issues as health care, the environment, human rights, economic competition and interdependence, age-old ethnic enmities, and political and military alliances. This theme typically appears in units or courses dealing with geography, culture, and economics but may also draw upon the natural and physical sciences and the humanities.

At the high school level, students are able to think systematically about personal, national, and global decisions, interactions, and consequences, including addressing critical issues such as peace, human rights, trade, and global ecology.

Civic Ideals and Practices

An understanding of civic ideals and practices of citizenship is critical to full participation in society and is a central purpose of the social studies. Students confront such questions as: What is civic participation and how can I be involved? How has the meaning of citizenship evolved? What is the balance between rights and responsibilities? What is the role of the citizen in the community and the nation, and as a member of the world community? How can I make a positive difference? In schools, this theme typically appears in units or courses dealing with history, political science, cultural anthropology, and fields such as global studies, law-related education, and the humanities.

High school students increasingly recognize the rights and responsibilities of citizens in identifying societal needs, setting directions for public policies, and working to support both individual dignity and the common good. They learn by experience how to participate in community service and political activities and how to use democratic process to influence public policy.

Foundational Skills[4]

The following foundational skills should apply to all students in all disciplines:

Communication. A process by which information is exchanged and a concept of "meaning" is being created and shared between individuals through a common system of symbols, signs, or behavior. Students should be able to communicate clearly, fluently, strategically, technologically, critically, and creatively in society and in a variety of workplaces. This process can best be accomplished through use of the following skills: reading, writing, speaking, listening, viewing, and visually representing.

Problem solving. The identification of an obstacle or challenge and the application of knowledge and thinking processes which include reasoning, decision making, and inquiry in order to reach a solution using multiple pathways, even when no routine path is apparent.

Resource access and utilization. The process of identifying, locating, selecting, and using resource tools to help in analyzing, synthesizing, and communicating information. The identification and employment of appropriate tools, techniques, and technologies are essential to all learning processes. These resource tools include pen, pencil, and paper; audio/video material, word processors, computers, interactive devices, telecommunication, and other emerging technologies.

Linking and generating knowledge. The effective use of cognitive processes to generate and link knowledge across the disciplines and in a variety of contexts. In order to engage in the principles of continual improvement, students must be able to transfer and elaborate on these processes. Transfer refers to the ability to apply a strategy or content knowledge effectively in a setting or context other than that in which it was originally learned. Elaboration refers to monitoring, adjusting, and expanding strategies into other contexts.

Citizenship. The application of the understanding of the ideals, rights, and responsibilities of active participation in a democratic republic that includes working respectfully and productively together for the benefit of the individual and the community; being accountable for one's choices and actions and understanding their impact on oneself and others; knowing one's civil, constitutional, and statutory rights; and mentoring others to be productive citizens and lifelong learners.

Information Literacy [5]

Students must become competent and independent users of information to be productive citizens of the twenty-first century. They must be prepared to live in an information-rich and changing global society. Due to the rapid growth of technology, the amount of information available is accelerating so quickly that teachers are no longer able to impart a complete knowledge base

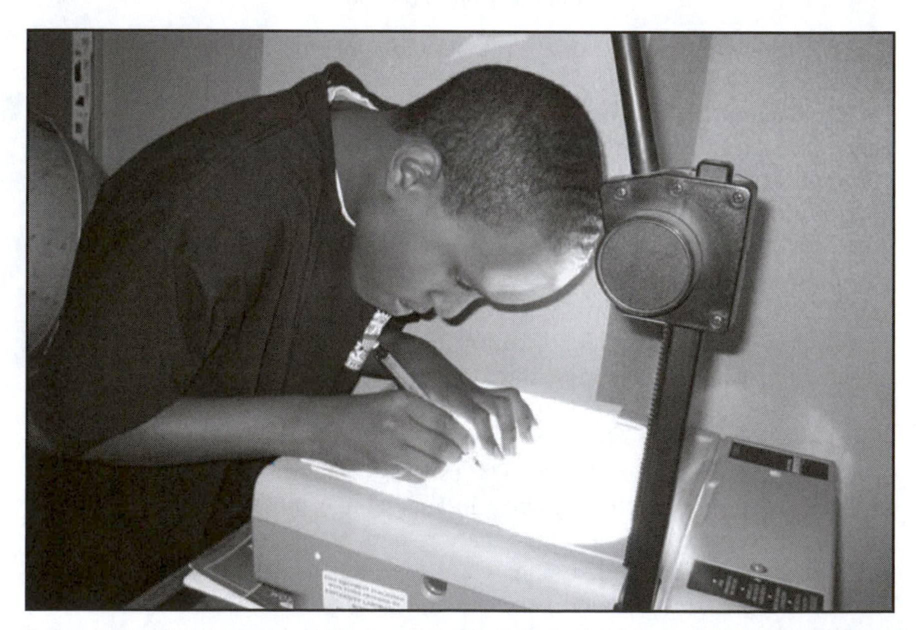

Information literacy is the ability to recognize an information need and then locate, evaluate, and effectively use the needed information.

in a subject area. In addition, students entering the workforce must know how to access information, solve problems, make decisions, and work as part of a team. Therefore, information literacy—the ability to recognize an information need and then locate, evaluate, and effectively use the needed information—is a basic skill essential to the twenty-first century workplace and home.

Information literate students are self-directed learners who, individually or collaboratively, use information responsibly to create quality products and to be productive citizens. Information literacy skills must not be taught in isolation; they must be integrated across all content areas, utilizing fully the resource of the classroom, the school library media center, and the community. The Information Literacy Model for Lifelong Learners (below) is a framework that teachers at all levels can apply to help students become independent life-long learners.

Defining/focusing. The first task is to recognize that an information need exists. Students make preliminary decisions about the type of information needed based on prior knowledge.

Selecting tools and resources. After students decide what information is needed, they then develop search strategies for locating and accessing appropriate, relevant sources in the school library media center, community libraries and agencies, resource people, and others as appropriate.

Extracting and recording. Students examine the resources for readability, currency, usefulness, and bias. This task involves skimming or listening for key words, "chunking" reading (chunking is a procedure of breaking up reading material into manageable sections), finding main ideas, and taking notes.

Processing information. After recording information, students must examine and evaluate the data in order to utilize the information retrieved. Students must interact with the information by categorizing, analyzing, evaluating, and comparing for bias, inadequacies, omissions, errors, and value judgments. Based on their findings, they either move on to the next step or do additional research.

Organizing information. Students effectively sort, manipulate, and organize the information that was retrieved. They make decisions on how to use and communicate their findings.

Presenting findings. Students apply and communicate what they have learned (e.g., research report, project, illustration, dramatization, portfolio, book, book report, map, oral/audio/visual presentation, game, bibliography, hyperstack).

Evaluating efforts. Throughout the information problem solving process, students evaluate their efforts. This assists students in determining the effectiveness of the research process. The final product may be evaluated by the teacher and also by other qualified or interested resource persons.

Notes

[1] Adapted from J. Stockard (2003), *Activities for Elementary School Social Studies*, 2nd ed. Long Grove, IL: Waveland Press.

[2] Adapted from National Council for the Social Studies (1989), Report of the Ad Hoc Committee on Scope and Sequence, 1988. *Social Education* 53(6):375. ©1997 National Council for the Social Studies. Used by permission.

[3] Adapted from the Louisiana State Department of Education (http://www.doe.state.la.us/lde/).

[4] Adapted from the Louisiana State Department of Education (http://www.doe.state.la.us/lde/). Note that these foundation skills are listed numerically in parentheses at the end of each benchmark (see Section V of this book).

[5] Adapted from the Louisiana State Department of Education (http://www.doe.state.la.us/lde/).

SECTION III

Planning for Secondary Social Studies

Lesson Planning

A first step in planning social studies lessons is to identify the major concepts to be stressed. These concepts are the big ideas of the social sciences: conflict, interdependence, change, scarcity, multiple causation, citizenship, justice, freedom, diversity, culture, resources, needs and wants, environment, authority/power, social control, and morality. A second step is to identify specific objectives—what students will learn from the lesson. At this point, the teacher asks, "What skills, attitudes, appreciations, understandings, or facts do I want the students to develop and/or refine through this lesson?"

Lesson Plan Format

With basic social science concepts and objectives in mind, the teacher designs the lesson. Here the work of Madeline Hunter is helpful. Hunter tells us that it is important to focus students' attention at the beginning of the lesson. For example, a teacher may focus attention by identifying a key word (such as *desert*) from the content to be studied and by asking students to think of three words or phrases that come to mind when they hear it. Volunteers write words on the board. Or a teacher may display a series of pictures relative to the topic to be studied and ask students to decide how they are the same. Or a teacher may play a recording of music that relates to the topic to be studied or share a poem. A teacher may even begin with a rapid review discussion. Generally a relatively brief segment of the lesson, this "anticipatory set" turns children on to what is to be learned and gets them ready to learn.

Hunter also suggests that in some cases it is wise to tell students what they will learn through the lesson or be able to do as a result of it. In essence, she is suggesting that the teacher communicate his or her objectives to the students and tell them why they are learning what they are learning. Establishing the anticipatory set and communicating the lesson objectives are the introduction to the lesson.

The next step in lesson preparation is deciding how instruction should proceed. The teacher must ask himself or herself, "What strategies will I use to achieve my objectives? How will I get my students actively involved in the major concepts and the content I want to teach?" The possibilities are endless. The teacher needs to see a direct connection between the strategies chosen and the objectives sought and that it is important to model the thinking processes that students will eventually use on their own. Simply making an assignment for students to complete is insufficient. There must be direct instruction and modeling of what is to be done.

As part of the direct instruction and modeling phase of the lesson, the teacher must check continuously for student understanding. The question for the teacher here is simple: "Are the students grasping the essence of what I am teaching?" Hunter proposes three techniques to check understanding: (1) asking a question of the group and getting an answer from one student as a

Box 3.1 Lesson Plan Format

Lesson Topic: (a descriptive title)

Grade Level & Subject: 0000
(grade level/subject for which the lesson is intended)

Time Allocated for Lesson: 0000
(How much time will this lesson take?)

Materials Needed:
(a list of the materials needed to teach the lesson)

1. 0000
2. 0000
3. 0000

Objectives: (These can be phrased from the grade-level expectations. Some will be behavioral; some will be general.)
As a result of this lesson, the learner will:

- 0000
- 0000
- 0000

Introduction:
(getting attention)

1. 0000
2. 0000
3. 0000
4. 0000

Major Instructional Sequence:
(e.g., modeling, giving instruction, explaining, visuals, audio, directing an activity, checking for understanding, guided practice)

1. 0000
2. 0000
3. 0000
4. 0000
5. 0000
6. 0000

Closure or Evaluation:
(how you will bring the lesson to a close)

1. 0000
2. 0000

sample of overall understanding; (2) asking a question and triggering a unison response, either oral or signaled by some hand motion; or (3) asking for an individual, private response through writing or drawing.

Hunter further suggests that the teacher schedule guided practice to make sure students know what they are to do if they are to work on the concept or skill on their own. Part of this guided practice should be an opportunity to review and conclude. Students should be asked to demonstrate their growing understanding or skill by identifying important points and big ideas or by recalling the steps in the procedure they will complete on their own. In essence, the teacher at this point is seeking closure, pulling the threads of the lesson together in what we might call its "concluding set." Once that is accomplished, the teacher may schedule independent work that will reinforce the learning sought.

In short, Hunter's design for effective lessons includes seven steps: (1) establishing an anticipatory set, (2) communicating the lesson's objective, (3) providing direct instruction, (4) modeling processes to be learned, (5) checking for understanding, (6) guiding practice so that it is meaningful, and (7) providing independent activity or practice. Not all seven steps appear in all lessons; the sequence may extend over several lessons, and the order of the steps should be varied to fit the needs of the students and the subject matter. Hunter suggests, however, that in planning lessons, the teacher should consider each of the seven elements and should think in terms of an anticipatory set, and instructional/modeling sequence, and a concluding set.

Pacing the Lesson[1]

Pacing is the speed at which the lesson proceeds. It is the rhythm, the ebb and flow, of a lesson.

- Develop awareness of your own teaching tempo. A good means of determining your pace is to audiotape or videotape your performance.
- Watch for nonverbal cues indicating that students are becoming puzzled or bored.
- Break activities up into short segments.
- Provide short breaks for lessons that last longer than 30 minutes. Long lessons can cause inattentiveness and disruptive behavior.
- Vary style as well as the content of the instruction. Students often become restless with only a single instructional approach.
- Avoid interrupting the flow of the lesson with numerous stops and starts. Jerkiness is a term that refers to behaviors that interfere with the smooth flow of the lesson. This occurs when the teacher (a) interrupts an ongoing activity without warning and gives directions to begin another activity; (b) leaves one activity dangling in midair and begins another, only to return to the first; or (c) leaves one activity for another and never returns to the first activity.

- Avoid slowdowns that interfere with the pace of the lesson. Slowdowns, or delays in the momentum or pace of a class, can occur due to "overdwelling" (spending too much time on directions or explanations) or fragmentation (dividing the lesson into such minute fragments that some of the students are left waiting and become bored).
- Provide a summary at the end of a lesson segment. Rather than a single summary at the end of the lesson, it might help the pacing to summarize after each main point or activity.

Internet Resources for Lesson Plans

- *PBS TeacherSource*
  More than 3,000 free lesson plans and activities.
  http://www.pbs.org/teachersource/soc_stud.htm
- *LessonPlansPage.com*
  An impressive and comprehensive assortment of unit and lesson plans.
  http://www.lessonplanspage.com/SSJH.htm
- *Lesson Plans and Resources for Social Studies Teachers*
  An award-winning site from a CSU–Northridge professor that includes lesson plans and teaching strategies, online activities, newsgroups and mailing lists, teaching current events, social studies school service, educational standards and curriculum frameworks, and more.
  http://www.csun.edu/~hcedu013/
- *InstructorWeb*
  A generous selection of printable lessons, lesson plans, and worksheets, all written by teachers.
  http://www.instructorweb.com/socialstudies.asp
- *Best of History Web Sites: Lesson Plans/Activities*
  An annotated listing of teacher-recommended Web sites for social studies lesson plans.
  http://www.besthistorysites.net/LessonPlans.shtml
- *Lesson Plans and Teaching Resources for Social Studies*
  http://www.csun.edu/~hcedu013/plans.html
- *The New York Times Learning Network on the Web*
  Teacher Connections, Grades 6–12
  Includes Learning at Home, Lesson Plan Archive, other lesson plan links and resources, Education News, Discussion Topics, Education Products, and more.
  Home page: http://www.nytimes.com/learning/ (includes searchable lesson plan database)
  Teacher connections: http://www.nytimes.com/learning/teacher

- *Newspapers in Education Online*
  Weekly and daily lesson plans incorporating current events.
  http://dnie.com/
- *Social Studies Lesson Plans*
  Hundreds of diverse, detailed lesson plans from Columbia Education Center.
  http://www.col-ed.org/cur/social.html

Planning Thematic Units

Thematic units are designed to study a topic in depth over an extended period of time, ranging from several days to several weeks. Teaching units are prepared for a particular class and are often in the form of a sequence of daily lesson plans. A unit usually includes the following sections:

Title. A topic or problem such as Life in Mexico City, Notable Battles of the Civil War, River Systems of North America, or Countries of the Arab World should appear on a cover page at the beginning of the unit.

Grade level and subject. An indication of the grade level (or grade levels) and subject for which the unit is designed. It is important to have this information on the title page so the grade level can be determined without hunting for it within the lesson plans.

Graphic organizer. A graphic representation of the unit on a single page (see pp. 75–78). It shows the theme of the unit at the center of a web and links

Figure 3.1 Parts of a Unit

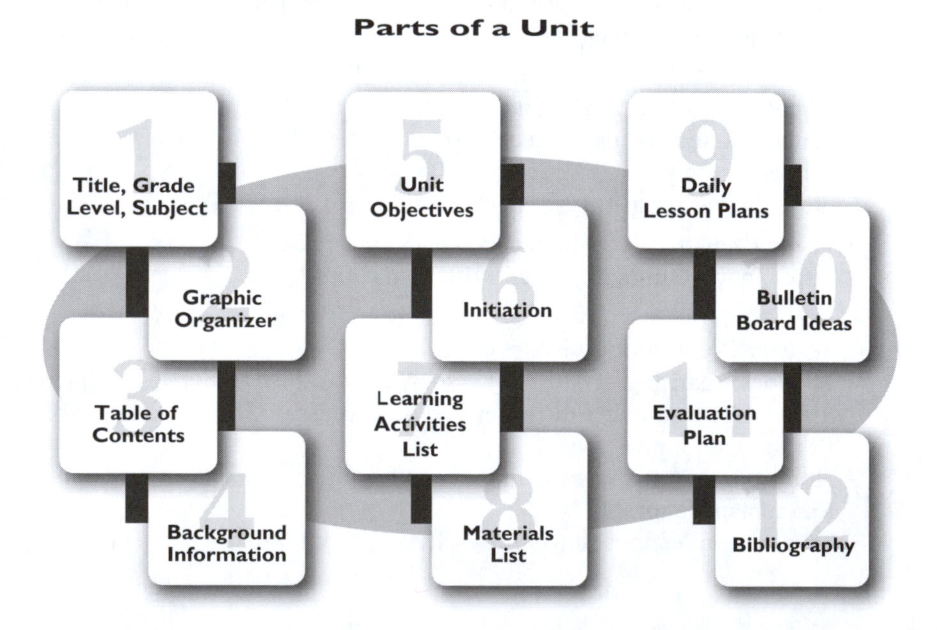

associating the theme with the various divisions and subdivisions of the unit. The graphic organizer is an important planning tool in designing the unit. It helps in dividing and subdividing the theme into manageable and logical areas of inquiry and study.

Table of contents. The directory that will guide the user to the various components of the unit. It should contain numbered pages (if the unit is hard copy) or hyperlinks (if the unit is on a Web site) and be placed right after the unit's graphic organizer.

Background information. A general overview of the unit's content, main ideas, and concepts is of unequivocal importance in bringing the teacher up to date on a unit that was prepared some months ago and is now being used, either for the first time or after a long delay. It also serves as the rationale for the unit. With the Internet sources available today, this section of the unit may very well contain Web pages replete with backup details and information for the unit.

Objectives. Although there are objectives for and within each lesson plan in the unit, there should be a separate page at the beginning of the unit depicting objectives for the unit as a whole—both behavioral and general—of expected knowledge, skill, or outcomes. These are objectives that would be met by the unit as a whole rather than by any one lesson plan. For example, a thematic unit on River Systems of North America might have a unit behavioral objective such as, "At the conclusion of this unit, the learner will locate on a map four of the rivers studied in this unit," or "At the conclusion of this unit, the learner will match the tributaries with the rivers into which they flow," or a general objective (which will not be accomplished in one lesson or one unit) such as "At the conclusion of this unit the learner will have a better appreciation for the beauty of rivers in North America." No one lesson in the unit addressed all of the information necessary to meet these objectives, but as a whole the lessons of the unit did address all of the information necessary to satisfy the objectives.

Initiation. Suggestions for beginning the unit are important. The class is going to engage the theme of the unit for a rather lengthy period of time, so the introduction of the unit should be done with some pizzazz—a motivational flair to arouse interest and kindle excitement about the pending period of inquiry and exploration.

List of learning activities. Although learning activities are fully described in each lesson plan, it is good to have a simple list of the various activities to be conducted in the lessons of the unit on a separate page at this point in the unit. This allows the user of the unit to glance at one page and get a sense of the types, number, and variety of activities included in the unit. If there is a field trip in a particular lesson, for example, it stands out well in advance at this point in the unit. In addition, the unit's activity balance will be evident: Are there introductory activities to focus attention on each main idea or problem to be investigated; developmental activities to provide for intake, organization, application, and expressions of content; and concluding activities to reemphasize main ideas, express ideas creatively, and culminate the unit?

List of materials needed for unit. This list should also appear separately, even though each lesson plan has its own list of materials needed. A master list of materials allows the user of the unit to do a quick assessment of the types of materials needed in the unit so that inventories can be checked in the school storeroom. The unit list of materials is not extensive or numerically exact; it is just a picture of the overall materials needed for the unit. If brown tempera paint is used in seven lessons, it's not listed seven times in the unit list—just a notation of "brown tempera paint."

Daily lesson plans. This is certainly the bulkiest part of the unit because it contains the plans for each lesson (see lesson planning earlier in this section). As a rule each lesson plan runs about 2 to 3 pages in length, and many units will have 8 to 12 lesson plans, so in terms of bulk the lesson plans can account for up to 36 or more pages in a unit.

Bulletin board sketches. During the course of creating a unit and developing lesson plans to explore its theme, many excellent ideas for bulletin boards will occur. This is the time to make simple sketches of these good bulletin-board ideas and insert them into the unit. Later, when it is time to implement the unit, these sketches will serve as reminders of appropriate bulletin boards that can be used to augment and enhance the implementation of the unit.

Evaluation. At this point in the creation of the unit, suggestions for assessment strategies, tests, and so on are placed in the unit. A written description of how learning progress and accomplishment will be assessed is placed at this point in the unit. It is important to include any tests prepared for the unit, along with test keys for those tests.

Bibliography. The bibliography for the thematic unit should be divided into two parts: one containing books for students and one containing professional books for the teacher. The books for students should be gathered based on the unit's theme and should represent many different reading levels. One of the wonderful attributes of children's literature is that there is a plethora of books available, written at differing reading levels, on any given topic. The student in grade 10 who reads at the third-grade level can have access to a book about Columbus, for example, with which he or she can succeed. According to Shirley Engle:[2]

1. *Units may be developed around current controversial problems.*

2. *Units may be developed around the basic needs for the satisfaction of which all cultures strive and around which all controversy has raged.* Such units might be entitled: How shall we feed, shelter, and clothe the people of the world? How shall we conserve and fully use the human and natural resources of the world? How shall we provide for the spiritual and aesthetic needs of the people of the world? How shall we provide for education and for the improvement of living throughout the world? How shall we organize for group living and personal security? Each of these titles implies an unfinished task and several possible courses of action based on differences in points of view.

3. *Units may be developed around the study of particular cultures.* Since the purpose of the culturally based units is to develop insight, the content would

be concerned not so much with events as with a people's beliefs and with the way in which they lived and met their basic needs.

4. *Units may be developed around the great and persisting issues that have confronted humankind throughout the ages.* Some of these might be individual freedom and security, the establishment of law and justice, the rights of labor, the relationship between the races of men, civil rights, the form of governments, the relationship between the governing and the governed, and the control of the world's resources and populating of its lands. Each of these issues could be the core for the development of a unit which would not only focus attention on a current controversial question but would afford a rich opportunity to consult the past experience of humankind in dealing with these issues and to study and evaluate the rationalizations by which people have defended courses of action with respect to these problems.

Planning Lessons for Multiple Intelligences

In breaking from the traditional theory that individuals have a single, quantifiable intelligence, Howard Gardner believed that the set of abilities which allow a person to solve problems or to fashion products that are valued in one or more of the world's cultures is the substance of intelligence. Instead of viewing "smartness" in terms of a score on a standardized test, Gardner saw intelligence as:

- The ability to solve problems that one encounters in real life.
- The ability to generate new problems to solve.
- The ability to make something or offer a service that is valued within one's culture.

In offering this refreshingly pragmatic definition of intelligence, Gardner revealed a wider family of human intelligences, which he called *multiple intelligences.* This broader view of cognitive functioning sharply contrasted with the unitary "dip-stick" model of intelligence (the IQ definition of intelligence) perceived as the norm throughout much of the world. It broadened one's notion of what it meant to be intelligent and opened the minds of educators as to how learning can be improved so that students can achieve more of their potential.

Using his biological and cultural research as a basis for his theory of multiple intelligences, Gardner formulated a list composed of eight intelligences (box 3.2).

In terms of classroom instruction, accepting Gardner's theory of multiple intelligences has several implications. Because all eight intelligences are needed to function in society, teachers should think of all intelligences as equally important. This is a grand departure from the traditional view of intelligence, in which strong emphasis was placed primarily on the verbal and mathematical intelligences. The implication, then, is that teachers should structure the presentation of material in a style that engages most or all of the

Box 3.2 Gardner's Multiple Intelligences

Verbal–Linguistic (word smart)—The ability to use words well in speaking or writing.

Logical–Mathematical (number smart)—The ability to use numbers and logical reasoning well.

Visual–Spatial (art smart)—The ability to perceive the visual world through sensitivity to color, lines, shapes, form, and space, and their relationships to one another.

Bodily–Kinesthetic (body smart)—The ability and expertise to use the body to communicate, produce things, demonstrate physically, achieve coordination, and have tactile perceptions.

Musical–Rhythmic (music smart)—The ability to perceive, transform, discriminate, and express musical and rhythmic forms.

Interpersonal (people smart)—The ability to be perceptive and to adapt accordingly, maintaining self-confidence and self-discipline.

Intrapersonal (self smart)—The ability to be self-reflective and self-aware, in tune with one's inner feelings, values, beliefs, and thinking processes.

Naturalist (nature smart)—The ability to notice patterns and characteristics in the natural environment, with the concurrent ability to categorize things in the natural world and be sensitive to one's surroundings.

multiple intelligences. Figure 3.2 contains a grid for incorporating the multiple intelligences into the lesson plan.

Constructivism

In today's educational community, a theory known as constructivism is perhaps the most widely accepted view of how children learn. It proposes that children must be active participants in the development of their own understanding. Kauchak and Eggen (1998) said that "the basic tenet of constructivism is the idea that learners develop their own understanding, and they develop understanding that makes sense to them; they don't 'receive' it from teachers or written materials" (p. 185).

Deeply rooted in the cognitive theories of Piaget (1977) that date from the 1960s, constructivism rejects the notion that students' minds are blank slates awaiting something to be imprinted. Instead, constructivism suggests that students help create their own knowledge through the basic mental activities of assimilation and accommodation.

Stemming from the view that the mind constantly changes its structure to help us make sense of things that we perceive, Piaget described the shifting modifications in the mind as assimilation and accommodation. When things are familiar to us and fit well with what we already know from our previously developed understanding, we fit the new experiences into our existing ideas. Piaget called this process *assimilation*. When new experiences or perceptions

Figure 3.2 Lesson Plan Grid for Multiple Intelligences

Lesson Topic & Time Needed	
Materials Needed	1. 2.
Objectives	At the conclusion of this lesson, the learner will: 1. 2.
Standards (Benchmarks)	1. 2.

Introductory Sequence

Major Instructional Sequence

Verbal-Linguistic Activities	**Logical-Mathematical Activities**	**Intrapersonal Activities**	**Interpersonal Activities**
How can I include reading, writing, and speaking?	How can I include numbers, classification, critical thinking, and calculations?	How can I include private learning time, reflection, and student choice?	How can I include group work, peer sharing, collaborative learning, and discussion?
Visual-Spatial Activities How can I include visuals, colors, art, graphs, pictures, maps, and globes?	**Musical-Rhythmic Activities** How can I include music, sounds, rhythms, and dance?	**Bodily-Kinesthetic Activities** How can I include movement, exercise, drama, and crafts?	**Naturalist Activities** How can I include opportunities that will increase sensitivity to the natural world?

Closure & Evaluation	

do not fit with what we already know, however, Piaget said that we must appease the dissonance within our minds by modifying the new experience to make it fit. Piaget called this modifying process *accommodation*, a shift in our cognitive framework which permits assimilation of the new experience. Knowledge is built up by the learner as existing ideas are expanded, elaborated, and changed to allow a new idea to fit.

In the constructivist approach, then, learners actively build their own understanding through reflective thought. Reflective thinking is stimulated as learners brainstorm in an environment of encouragement (provided by the teacher), exploring the networks of ideas already existing in their minds. They integrate these networks, both within their own minds and by sharing with other learners through active reflective thought; they collaborate. The networks of ideas change, become rearranged, take on additions, and are modified as learning occurs. The more connections the learner can make with his or her existing network of ideas, the better that new experiences and ideas are understood (or learned).

Constructivist instruction is based on the supposition that the pupil is a naturally active learner who constructs new individual knowledge through linking prior knowledge with new knowledge. Constructivist learning involves an interactive and collaborative dialogue between the teacher, the pupil, and other learners. The teacher orchestrates the learning by providing a rich and supportive environment where assistance and direction allow the learner to construct his/her own knowledge. This construction of knowledge

According to constructivist theory, learners build their own understanding, linking prior knowledge with new knowledge through reflective thought.

results in ownership by the learner and, thus, a deeper understanding of the new information. The teacher focuses on guiding the learner to achieve success. The learner is a proactive participant in the learning process and not a sponge waiting to absorb knowledge.

Constructivist learning activities often begin with a question or a problem that can be pursued in a cooperative, collaborative group setting. The problem serves as a catalyst for motivation because it activates the learners' curiosity in an authentic way. (An authentic task in the classroom is one that requires thinking, understanding, and collaborative problem solving similar to what might be required in the real world outside the classroom.) Social interaction occurs as pupils verbalize and refine their thinking and understanding with other pupils in a collaborative process. New learning is rendered from the group's examination of content material and their social interaction in the context of their current understandings and existing knowledge.

Maslow's Hierarchy of Human Needs[3]

Abraham Harold Maslow (1908–1970) was born April 1, 1908, in Brooklyn, New York, and became a noted psychologist. Early in his career, one of the many interesting things Maslow noticed in his research with monkeys was that some needs take precedence over others. For example, if you are hungry and thirsty, you will tend to try to take care of the thirst first. After all, you can do without food for weeks, but you can only do without water for a couple of days! Thirst is a "stronger" need than hunger. Likewise, if you are very, very thirsty, but someone has put a choke hold on you and you can't breathe, which is more important? The need to breathe, of course.

Maslow took this idea and created his now famous *hierarchy of human needs* (see figure 3.3). Beyond the primary requirements of air, water, and food, he laid out five broader layers: the physiological needs, the needs for safety and security, the needs for love and belonging, the needs for esteem, and the need to actualize the self, in that order.

Physiological needs. These include the needs we have for oxygen, water, protein, salt, sugar, calcium, and other minerals and vitamins. They also include the need to maintain a pH balance (getting too acidic or base will kill you) and a "normal" temperature (98.6 or near to it). Also in this category are the needs to be active, to rest, to sleep, to get rid of bodily wastes, to avoid pain, and to have sex. Quite a collection! Maslow believed, and research supports him, that these are in fact individual needs, and that a lack of, say, vitamin C will lead to a very specific craving for things which have in the past provided that vitamin C—for example, orange juice.

Safety and security needs. When the physiological needs are largely taken care of, this second layer of needs comes into play. You will become increasingly interested in finding safe circumstances, stability, and protection. You might develop a need for structure, for order, some limits. Looking at it nega-

Figure 3.3 Maslow's Hierarchy of Human Needs

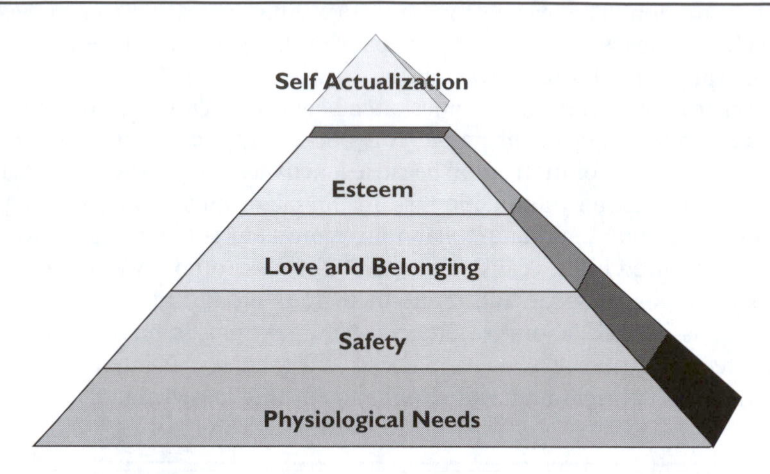

tively, you become concerned not with needs like hunger and thirst, but instead with your fears and anxieties. In the ordinary American adult, this set of needs manifest themselves in the form of our urges to have a home in a safe neighborhood, a little job security and a nest egg, a good retirement plan, a bit of insurance, and so on.

Love and belonging needs. When physiological needs and safety needs are by and large taken care of, a third layer takes the foreground. You begin to feel the need for friends, a sweetheart, children, affectionate relationships in general, even a sense of community. Looked at negatively, you become increasingly susceptible to loneliness and social anxieties. In our day-to-day life, we exhibit these needs in our desires to marry; to have a family; to be a part of a community, a member of a church, a brother in the fraternity, a part of a gang or a bowling club. It is also a part of what we look for in a career.

Esteem needs. Next, we begin to look for a little self-esteem. Maslow noted two versions of esteem needs, a lower one and a higher one. The lower one is the need for the respect of others, the need for status, fame, glory, recognition, attention, reputation, appreciation, dignity, even dominance. The higher form involves the need for self-respect, including such feelings as confidence, competence, achievement, mastery, independence, and freedom. Note that this is the "higher" form because, unlike the respect of others, once you have self-respect, it's a lot harder to lose!

Maslow calls all of the preceding four levels *deficit needs*, or *D-needs*. If you don't have enough of something—when you have a deficit—you feel the need. But if you get all you need, you feel nothing at all! In other words, the needs cease to be motivating. As the old blues song goes, "You don't miss your water till your well runs dry!"

He also talks about these levels in terms of *homeostasis*. Homeostasis is the principle by which your furnace thermostat operates: When it gets too cold, it switches the heat on; when it gets too hot, it switches the heat off. In the same way, your body, when it lacks a certain substance, develops a craving for it; when it gets enough of it, then the need stops. Maslow simply extends the homeostatic principle to needs, such as safety, belonging, and esteem, that we don't ordinarily think of in these terms.

Maslow sees all these needs as essentially survival needs. Even love and esteem are needed for the maintenance of health. He says we all have these needs built into us genetically, like instincts. In fact, he calls them *instinctoid* (instinct-like) needs.

Self-actualization. The last level is a bit different. Maslow has used a variety of terms to refer to this level: *growth motivation* (in contrast to deficit motivation), *being needs* (or *B-needs*, in contrast to D-needs), and *self-actualization*. These needs do not involve balance or homeostasis. Once engaged, they continue to be felt—in fact, they are likely to become stronger as we "feed" them. They involve the continuous desire to fulfill potentials, to "be all that you can be." They are a matter of becoming the most complete, the fullest, "you"—hence the term self-actualization.

In keeping with Maslow's theory up to this point, if you want to be truly self-actualizing, you need to have your lower needs taken care of, at least to a considerable extent. This makes sense: If you are hungry, you are scrambling to get food; If you are unsafe, you have to be continuously on guard; If you are isolated and unloved, you have to satisfy that need; If you have a low sense of self-esteem, you have to be defensive or compensate. When lower needs are unmet, you can't fully devote yourself to fulfilling your potential.

Maslow's hierarchy is important to teachers because it is at the level of self-actualization that students engage in learning activities. It is important for teachers to know if any unmet needs are interfering with a student's learning activities. Among other things, Maslow determined that self-actualizers have driving needs to be fully self-actualized and happy. Among those needs, he listed:

- *Truth* rather than dishonesty
- *Goodness* rather than evil
- *Beauty* rather than ugliness or vulgarity
- *Unity, wholeness, and transcendence of opposites* rather than arbitrariness or forced choices
- *Aliveness* rather than deadness or the mechanization of life
- *Uniqueness* rather than bland uniformity
- *Perfection and necessity* rather than sloppiness, inconsistency, or accident
- *Completion* rather than incompleteness
- *Justice and order* rather than injustice and lawlessness
- *Simplicity* rather than unnecessary complexity
- *Richness* rather than environmental impoverishment

- *Effortlessness* rather than strain
- *Playfulness* rather than grim, humorless drudgery
- *Self-sufficiency* rather than dependency
- *Meaningfulness* rather than senselessness

Questions in the Classroom

Questioning is one of the most popular modes of teaching. In 1912, a researcher stated that approximately 80 percent of a teacher's school day was spent asking questions of students. More contemporary research on teacher questioning behaviors and patterns indicate that this has not changed. Teachers today ask 300–400 questions each day.

Teachers ask questions for several reasons:

- The act of asking questions helps teachers keep students actively involved in lessons.
- While answering questions, students have the opportunity to openly express their ideas and thoughts.
- Questioning students enables other students to hear different explanations of the material by their peers.
- Asking questions helps teachers to pace their lessons and moderate student behavior.
- Questioning students helps teachers to evaluate student learning and revise their lessons as necessary.

For thousands of years, teachers have known that it is possible to transfer factual knowledge and conceptual understanding through the process of asking questions. As teachers, we ask many questions to find out what a learner knows and to encourage thinking. Unfortunately, although the act of asking questions has the potential to greatly facilitate the learning process, it also has the capacity to turn a child off to learning if done incorrectly.

Bloom's Taxonomy of Educational Objectives

Benjamin Bloom's *Taxonomy of Educational Objectives* (figure 3.4) provides us with a convenient framework for developing a solid questioning strategy.

- It is hierarchical in that the upper levels are dependent on and encompass the lower levels.
- Questions at the lower level require answers based on knowledge, whereas those at the higher levels require the application of knowledge and higher-order thinking skills.
- Questions which ask *who–what–when–where* often converge on a single answer and reside at the lowest level of Bloom's Taxonomy, the simple recall, knowledge level.

Figure 3.4 Bloom's Taxonomy

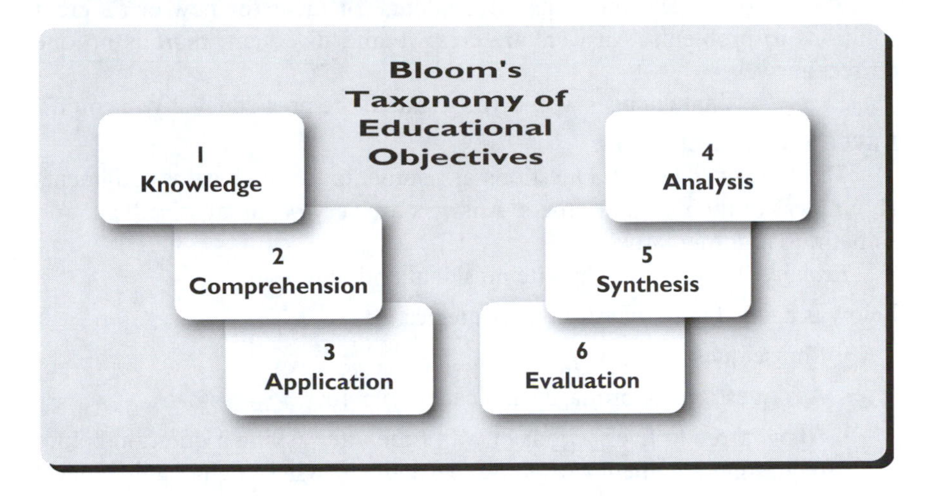

- Questions which ask *why* and *how*, however, are frequently divergent questions with several possible correct answers which engage the respondent in higher-order thinking. Such questions reside at the higher levels of Bloom's Taxonomy.
- It is important for teachers to use questions that range up and down Bloom's Taxonomy and not stay at the simple recall, knowledge level too much of the time.

Following is a description of the levels within Bloom's Taxonomy.

LEVEL ONE—KNOWLEDGE

The Level of Simple Recall. Questions ask for factual information and answers are either right or wrong.

Example: Who was the first American president?

LEVEL TWO—COMPREHENSION

The Level of Understanding. Questions ask for reasons; answers are usually right or wrong.

Example: What do you think the president does?

LEVEL THREE—APPLICATION

The Level of Usage. Questions usually ask for ways to use knowledge and allow for individual creativity. There may be more than one correct answer.

Example: How can we select a class president?

LEVEL FOUR—ANALYSIS

The Level of Relationships and Intent. Questions ask for comparisons to be made or for component parts of an idea. Answers are more divergent and personal.

Example: How does the role of the British prime minister compare to that of the president of the United States?

Level Five—Synthesis

The Level of Ideas. Questions ask students for ideas for new or different solutions to problems. Answers are creative and divergent; there is no one correct answer.

Example: What changes would you make in the presidency if you could?

Level Six—Evaluation

The Level of Judgment. Questions ask students to make value judgments about ideas of their own or others. Answers are very personal, divergent, and sometimes argumentative.

Example: Who is your favorite president and why?

Below is a list of good questioning strategies.

- Phrase questions clearly.
- Ask questions of primarily an academic nature.
- Allow three to five seconds of wait time after asking a question before requesting a student's response, particularly when high-cognitive level questions are asked.
- Encourage students to respond in some way to each question asked.
- Balance responses from volunteering and non-volunteering students.
- Elicit a high percentage of correct responses from students and tactfully assist with incorrect responses.
- Probe students' responses in order to have them clarify ideas, support a point of view, or extend their thinking; acknowledge correct responses from students and use praise specifically and discriminately.

Group Work, Collaboration, and Cooperative Learning

Working in groups provides students with unparalleled learning experiences that allow them to experience the rewards of collaborative problem solving (where students work and think jointly) in a cooperative environment (where students concur in their efforts). Pursuing a task or seeking a solution to a problem as a member of a group provides the elementary social studies pupil with three distinct and rewarding opportunities:

- It emulates the real world in the sense that companies establish work-teams to solve problems.
- It gives students an opportunity to collaborate cognitively in the pursuit of a task or a problem.
- It provides opportunities for unsurpassed social interaction.

Providing students with opportunities to become actively involved in their learning tasks can be one of the most productive endeavors in the secondary social studies classroom. Group work is a major way to engage stu-

Collaborative group work is a significant way in which to engage students in hands-on, student-participatory learning experiences.

dents in hands-on, pupil-participatory learning experiences that are both instructionally beneficial and highly motivational. The task itself provides a cognitive focus for the members of the group, and the ensuing student interactions yield many opportunities for collaboration, problem solving, and cooperative learning.

Principal approaches relating to group work are known by different labels: cooperative learning, student team learning, group investigation, and collaborative learning. While each of these approaches may differ in certain aspects of learning and instructional design, such as group structure and teacher role, there are certain attributes that are considered common to all group learning approaches.

Working in Pairs

Arranging students into pairs is a good place to start when you are introducing your students to group work. It is the simplest form of group work and the easiest kind of group work to manage. Simple pairing involves organizing students into pairs and giving each pair a task. One idea is to encourage students to think about content, compare their thoughts with those of their partners (collaboration), and share their responses with the whole group. An excellent pairing activity for social studies involves giving each pair a laminated desk map (Nystrom, Cram, or equivalent) so they can locate coordinates of latitude and longitude. This can be done in several formats:

- Provide each pair with a list of coordinates to locate.
- Provide each pair with an imaginary ship's itinerary where coordinates are given for the ship's origination point, several stops along the way, and a final destination. (For more mature students, this may become a long-term collaboration in which they also do research on what products the ship might be delivering and acquiring at each stop, plus information about the places themselves, such as geography, history, government, and so on.)
- Each pair is given a list of cities (or countries) for which they are to supply the coordinates.
- Each pair constructs a list of coordinates (cities, countries, or ship's itinerary) to be solved by another pair group but checked by the pair group that created the task.
- A competition can be held in which the teacher calls out a coordinate (or a city or a country) and the pair groups collaborate quickly to see which group can be first to respond correctly.

Working in Larger Groups

While grouping in pairs is a good place to begin when you are introducing your students to group work, there are times when you may want students to work in groups of three, four, or five. Groups larger than five are generally unwieldy and are not recommended. One distinct advantage of having students work in groups of three, four, or five is the opportunity to promote additional social skills while cooperating and collaborating in pursuit of the cognitive goals of the task at hand. In larger groups, students can experience practice in fulfilling different group roles, like being the group leader or other specific roles, such as researcher, scribe, spokesperson, facilitator, artist, and so on.

One simple way to initiate group work in larger groups is to combine pairs. As students experience group work activities in pairs, it is a simple matter to combine pairs to form groups of four, retaining the simplicity of pairing yet promoting the social skill development available when students work in larger groups. A good activity for demonstrating the transition from group work in pairs to group work in larger groups (combined pairs) would be the imaginary ship's itinerary described above. Once pairs had found the coordinates for the ship's origination point, several stops along the way, and final destination, larger groups could be formed by combining pairs to do research on what products the ship might be delivering and acquiring at each stop, along with information about the geography, history, government, etc., of the places along the route. The larger groups would experience more social interaction and group members would take on specific and designated responsibilities for the group's mission.

It is important for the teacher to have a procedure for dividing the class into groups, and it is important for the class to understand (and practice) the procedure until it becomes a well-known routine. For spontaneous grouping, the procedure might simply be to have students count off by fives or sixes (for example, 1-2-3-4-5, 1-2-3-4-5, 1-2-3-4-5, etc.) until all students are numbered. Then, simply say, "All ones group at this table, all twos group at this table . . ." and so on. Often, teachers will have the class sit in groupings of about five, joining their desks together to form a sort of table for the group. These semi-permanent groups, then, can often work together as they are seated. At other times they can be divided, as in the 1-2-3-4-5 scheme, and at still other times they may be divided because of task selection reasons (as in grouping to work on a unit in which each student has selected one of the unit's major components on which to work).

Other reasons for organizing students into temporary groups might include common needs, like the aggressive reteaching of undeveloped skills (for example, students who still cannot find coordinates of latitude and longitude while most members of the class can, or students who do not understand the consequences of the tilt, rotation, and revolution of the Earth when it is common knowledge for most of the class members), students who are grouped together because of their talents (an artist, an articulate speaker, a good reader, and the like), and students who are grouped together for social reasons (Jennifer, Trey, and Renee like to work together and work particularly well together).

Group work is an effective strategy for promoting and maintaining high levels of student involvement because it engages students in tasks to be solved in a group. Combined with skilled questioning, grouping can help students develop social skills and promote the development of higher-order thinking skills.

While group work can enhance both social interaction and cognitive learning through higher-order thinking skills and problem solving, it is important for the teacher to ensure that all members of the group participate. Often, lower achievers or less aggressive members of the group defer to the higher achievers or more aggressive members of the group. While there is no simple answer to this problem, teachers can encourage equal participation by circulating around the room and closely monitoring the groups, frequently checking for individual understanding, and providing individual assistance as needed; by strategically calling on non-volunteers in a group; and by reminding the groups that all group members need to understand the group's thinking in solving problems.

Collaboration and Cooperative Learning

In its purest sense, collaboration means to labor together, especially in an intellectual endeavor. When social studies students are engaged in collaborative, cooperative group work, they work jointly with others to solve problems, complete tasks, unravel puzzles, probe resources, collect and analyze data, and so on. They utilize information literacy together and concurrently (information literacy being the process that students develop to find and use information—see pp. 50–51).

Let's say your class is studying the problems associated with cutting trees from the rain forest. You might form students into collaborative, cooperative groups, giving each pupil an authentic role (for example, that of a biologist, a geographer, an economist, an environmentalist, a botanist). As students gather data and information related to their roles and to the problem at hand, they collaborate in a variety of ways. They share information, they brainstorm, and they investigate multiple resources (including CD-ROM reference tools, Web sites, nonfiction books, and maps). Students' abilities to communicate, solve problems, and exercise appropriate social skills (sociability that includes being empathetic, responsive, and accommodating) are essential components of collaboration. The ability to access information efficiently and apply it to decision making and problem solving are keys to success in our world of rapidly growing information. Information literacy, then, is a basic survival skill for today's students. And information literacy is developed, nurtured, and optimized through collaborative, cooperative learning experiences. The collaborative, cooperative experience makes learning:

- *meaningful*, because its application is explicit;
- *authentic*, because there is connectedness to the real world where higher-order thinking and depth are important; and
- *application-oriented*, because students have experiences in applying what they learn to a variety of contexts so that the transfer of learning from one situation to another is implicit.

Developing the ability to find and use information, and reaching a level of independence and social responsibility to make appropriate use of that ability, qualifies one as *information literate*. Collaboration helps students see the connections between learning processes and how to apply them to problem-solving and decision-making situations. Information literacy cannot be developed and nurtured in isolation, but rather needs meaningful and authentic application, the kind we find in collaborative, cooperative group work.

An important element of collaborative, cooperative learning is individual accountability. Each member of the group must learn the subject matter or complete the task and be evaluated on his or her performance. It is presumed that all students in the group will make distinct contributions to the task at hand and that no one group member has all the answers or does all of the thinking. They are all members of the group, and each person is dependent on the other group members. The group is united in a common purpose to complete a task, utilizing the efforts of every member of the group. Students directly interact with each other in a collaborative manner in pursuing the group's task, and accountability is often determined by teacher evaluation of group work and the group's presentation of its findings.

Cooperative learning has potential as a powerful teaching strategy in secondary classrooms, impacting both academic and social skills. Cooperative group work creates new opportunities for students to respond and practice new skills by allowing them to learn through interactions with their peers. In addition, teachers can improve their ability to individualize work for a wide range of students with varying abilities by focusing on a handful of groups instead of myriad individuals. Although obstacles to the positive functioning of cooperative learning groups in secondary classrooms are plentiful, success is possible for teachers who implement the strategy with thoughtfulness and care.

Graphic Organizers and Concept Mapping

Graphic organizers are visual representations that help students organize, study, and remember material. Sometimes called *semantic maps* or *concept maps*, graphic organizers are especially useful in assisting students in understanding social studies textbooks and nonfiction informational books and resources. They help students to focus their attention on important features and to become organized thinkers. In demonstrating the use of graphic organizers to students, the teacher may read a few passages from a social studies book, reference, or nonfiction informational book and use the overhead projector, computer projection, or chalkboard to organize the material graphically, soliciting student help and input in the process. Students might then practice the technique in small, collaborative groups with different sections from the textbook, a reference material, an Internet resource, or a nonfiction informational book.

The graphic organizer is composed of a central idea, with spokes going out to several main topics which have details nested beneath them. Figure 3.5 shows a sample graphic organizer of a unit featuring the Middle East as the central idea; the main topics are countries, economics, languages, religions, government, geography, history, and holidays; and details will be nested beneath the main topics.

Concept mapping is a graphical system for understanding the relationship between concepts (ideas). Representing knowledge in the visual format of a concept map allows one to gain an overview of a domain of knowledge. Because the nodes contain only a keyword or a short sentence, more interpretation is required of the reader, but this may be positive. Concept mapping can be used for several purposes:

- to generate ideas (brainstorming);
- to design complex structures (long texts, hypermedia, large Web sites);
- to communicate complex ideas;
- to aid learning by explicitly integrating new and old knowledge; and
- to assess understanding or diagnose misunderstanding.

Figure 3.5 Graphic Organizer for a Unit

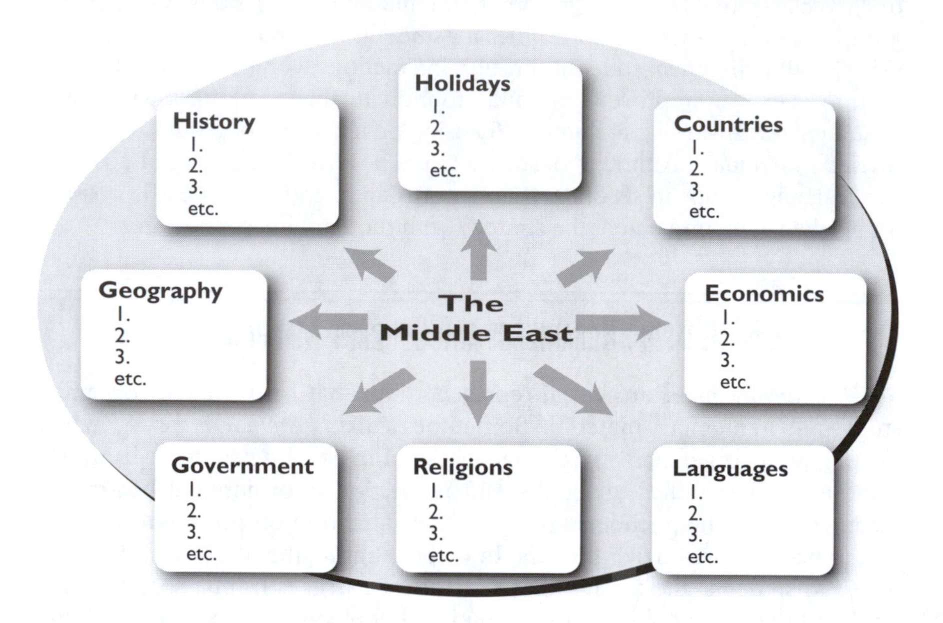

Visual representation via concept maps has several advantages:

- visual symbols are quickly and easily recognized;
- minimum use of text makes it easy to scan for a word, phrase, or the general idea; and
- visual representation allows for development of a holistic understanding that words alone cannot convey.

Concept mapping has many applications. Among the uses of concept mapping are:

Creativity tool. Drawing a concept map can be compared to participating in a brainstorming session. As one puts ideas down on paper without criticism, the ideas become clearer and the mind becomes free to receive new ideas. These new ideas may be linked to ideas already on the paper, and they may also trigger new associations leading to new ideas.

Hypertext design tool. As the World Wide Web becomes an increasingly powerful and ubiquitous medium for disseminating information, writers must move from writing text in linear fashion to creating hypertext documents with links to other documents. The structural correspondence between hypertext design and concept maps makes concept mapping a suitable tool for designing the conceptual structure of hypertext.

Communication tool. A concept map produced by one person represents one possible way to structure information or ideas. This is something that can be shared with others. A concept map produced by a group of people represents the ideas of the group. In either case, concept mapping can be a communication tool that people use to discuss concepts and the relationships between the concepts.

Learning tool. Constructivist learning theory argues that new knowledge should be integrated into existing structures in order to be remembered and receive meaning. Concept mapping stimulates this process by making it explicit and requiring the learner to pay attention to the relationship between concepts. Students demonstrate some of their best thinking when they try to represent something graphically, and thinking is a necessary condition for learning.

Problem-solving tool. Concept mapping is gaining inroads as a tool for problem solving in education. Concept mapping may be used to enhance the problem-solving phases of generating alternative solutions and options. Since problem solving in education is usually done in small groups, learning should also benefit from the communication enhancing properties of concept mapping.

Assessment tool. An important by-product of concept mapping is its ability to detect or illustrate the misconceptions learners may have. Concept maps drawn by students express their conceptions (or their misconceptions) and can help the teacher diagnose the misconceptions and provide more effective instruction in the future.

One of the best computer programs for constructing graphic organizers and concept maps is *Inspiration* (http://www.inspiration.com/—A free trial version of Inspiration software is available at the Web site). Organization of concepts, and brainstorming and mapping of ideas are mentioned in the User's Manual as primary functions of this program. The capabilities of Inspiration make it an outstanding program for creating graphs for presentation purposes. Nodes may be shown in many different useful preset and user-defined shapes. Links may be straight or curved and may be labeled. Arrowheads may be placed on any side, and everything may be set to any color. It encourages users to revise or change the maps (compared to maps drawn with paper and pencil). The graphical capabilities of Inspiration help users personalize concept maps. These capabilities also provide an incentive for users to manipulate concepts and revise conceptual relationships. Figure 3.6 on p. 78 shows what a concept map constructed with Inspiration software might look like.

Notes

[1] Adapted from Paul R. Burden & David M. Byrd (2003), *Methods of Effective.* Boston: Allyn & Bacon.

[2] Adapted from Shirley H. Engle (1949), Controversial Issues in World History Classes, in Edith West, ed., *Improving the teaching of world history.* Washington, DC: The National Council for the Social Studies, pp. 145–52.

[3] Adapted from C. George Boeree (2006), *Abraham Maslow.* Used by permission.

Figure 3.6 Concept Map

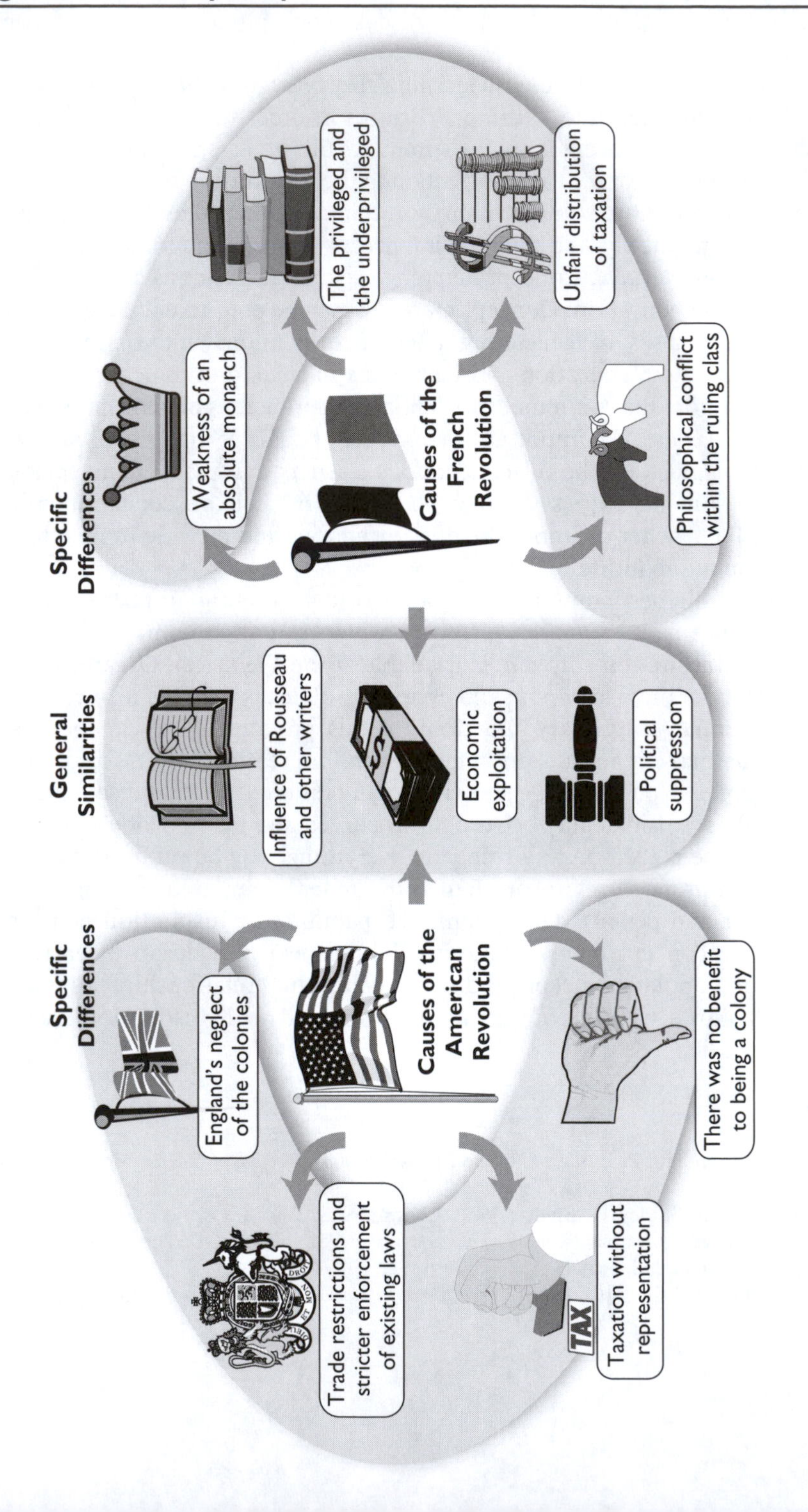

Section IV

INTASC Standards
An Umbrella for Evaluation

The Council of Chief State School Officers (CCSSO) is a nationwide, nonprofit organization of public officials who head departments of elementary and secondary education in the states, the District of Columbia, the Department of Defense Education Activity, and five U.S. extra-state jurisdictions. CCSSO provides leadership, advocacy, and technical assistance on major educational issues. The Council seeks members' consensus on major educational issues and expresses their views to civic and professional organizations, federal agencies, Congress, and the public.

The Interstate New Teacher Assessment and Support Consortium (INTASC)—a CCSSO-sponsored program—is a consortium of state education agencies and national educational organizations dedicated to the reform of the preparation, licensing, and ongoing professional development of teachers. Created in 1987, INTASC's primary constituency is state education agencies responsible for teacher licensing, program approval, and professional development. Its work is guided by one basic premise: An effective teacher must be able to integrate content knowledge with the specific strengths and needs of students to assure that *all* students learn and perform at high levels.

INTASC Standards

Various committees of practicing teachers, teacher educators, school leaders, and state agency staff crafted INTASC's standards, which articulate what all beginning teachers should know and be able to do to teach effectively. The various committees' missions were to take the INTASC core standards and translate them into appropriate policy for the teacher licensing system, specifically into licensing standards for individual candidates and standards for institutions that provide pre-service and in-service programs. These committees worked from existing documents of the various professional associations, particularly with recommended subject area standards for P–12 students. The purpose of this work was not to create yet another standards document, but to consider the best thinking of education practitioners and researchers, and to articulate the collective voice of the states regarding sound teacher licensing policy.

INTASC's *Model Standards for Beginning Teacher Licensing, Assessment and Development: A Resource for State Dialogue* (1992) outline the knowledge, dispositions, and performances deemed essential for all teachers regardless of the subject or grade level being taught. Drafted by a committee of teachers, teacher educators, and state agency officials, they represent a shared view among the states and within the profession of what constitutes competent beginning teaching.

An important attribute of these proposed standards is that they are *performance-based:* that is, *they describe what teachers should know and be able to do* rather than listing courses that teachers should take in order to be awarded a license. The standards are based on five assumptions about teachers:

1. Teachers are committed to students and their learning.
2. Teachers know the subjects they teach and how to teach those subjects to diverse learners.
3. Teachers are responsible for managing and monitoring student learning.
4. Teachers think systematically about their practice and learn from experience.
5. Teachers are members of learning communities.

Principle #1 *The teacher understands the central concepts, tools of inquiry, and structures of the discipline(s) he or she teaches and can create learning experiences that make these aspects of subject matter meaningful for students.*

Knowledge

- The teacher understands major concepts, assumptions, debates, processes of inquiry, and ways of knowing that are central to the discipline(s) s/he teaches.
- The teacher understands how students' conceptual frameworks and their misconceptions for an area of knowledge can influence their learning.
- The teacher can relate his/her disciplinary knowledge to other subject areas.

Dispositions

- The teacher realizes that subject matter knowledge is not a fixed body of facts but is complex and ever-evolving. S/he seeks to keep abreast of new ideas and understandings in the field.
- The teacher appreciates multiple perspectives and conveys to learners how knowledge is developed from the vantage point of the knower.
- The teacher has enthusiasm for the discipline(s) s/he teaches and sees connections to everyday life.
- The teacher is committed to continuous learning and engages in professional discourse about subject matter knowledge and children's learning of the discipline.

Performances

- The teacher effectively uses multiple representations and explanations of disciplinary concepts that capture key ideas and link them to students' prior understandings.
- The teacher can represent and use differing viewpoints, theories, "ways of knowing" and methods of inquiry in his/her teaching of subject matter concepts.
- The teacher can evaluate teaching resources and curriculum materials for their comprehensiveness, accuracy, and usefulness for representing particular ideas and concepts.

- The teacher engages students in generating knowledge and testing hypotheses according to the methods of inquiry and standards of evidence used in the discipline.
- The teacher develops and uses curricula that encourage students to see, question, and interpret ideas from diverse perspectives.
- The teacher can create interdisciplinary learning experiences that allow students to integrate knowledge, skills, and methods of inquiry from several subject areas.

Principle #2 *The teacher understands how children learn and develop, and can provide learning opportunities that support their intellectual, social and personal development.*

Knowledge

- The teacher understands how learning occurs—how students construct knowledge, acquire skills, and develop habits of mind—and knows how to use instructional strategies that promote student learning.
- The teacher understands that students' physical, social, emotional, moral and cognitive development influence learning and knows how to address these factors when making instructional decisions.
- The teacher is aware of expected developmental progressions and ranges of individual variation within each domain (physical, social, emotional, moral and cognitive), can identify levels of readiness in learning, and understands how development in any one domain may affect performance in others.

Dispositions

- The teacher appreciates individual variation within each area of development, shows respect for the diverse talents of all learners, and is committed to help them develop self-confidence and competence.
- The teacher is disposed to use students' strengths as a basis for growth, and their errors as an opportunity for learning.

Performances

- The teacher assesses individual and group performance in order to design instruction that meets learners' current needs in each domain (cognitive, social, emotional, moral, and physical) and that leads to the next level of development.
- The teacher stimulates student reflection on prior knowledge and links new ideas to already familiar ideas, making connections to students' experiences, providing opportunities for active engagement, manipulation, and testing of ideas and materials, and encouraging students to assume responsibility for shaping their learning tasks.
- The teacher accesses students' thinking and experiences as a basis for instructional activities by, for example, encouraging discussion, listen-

ing and responding to group interaction, and eliciting samples of student thinking orally and in writing.

Principle #3 *The teacher understands how students differ in their approaches to learning and creates instructional opportunities that are adapted to diverse learners.*

Knowledge

- The teacher understands and can identify differences in approaches to learning and performance, including different learning styles, multiple intelligences, and performance modes, and can design instruction that helps use students' strengths as the basis for growth.
- The teacher knows about areas of exceptionality in learning—including learning disabilities, visual and perceptual difficulties, and special physical or mental challenges.
- The teacher knows about the process of second language acquisition and about strategies to support the learning of students whose first language is not English.
- The teacher understands how students' learning is influenced by individual experiences, talents, and prior learning, as well as language, culture, family and community values.
- The teacher has a well-grounded framework for understanding cultural and community diversity and knows how to learn about and incorporate students' experiences, cultures, and community resources into instruction.

Dispositions

- The teacher believes that all children can learn at high levels and persists in helping all children achieve success.
- The teacher appreciates and values human diversity, shows respect for students' varied talents and perspectives, and is committed to the pursuit of "individually configured excellence."
- The teacher respects students as individuals with differing personal and family backgrounds and various skills, talents, and interests.
- The teacher is sensitive to community and cultural norms.
- The teacher makes students feel valued for their potential as people, and helps them learn to value each other.

Performances

- The teacher identifies and designs instruction appropriate to students' stages of development, learning styles, strengths, and needs.
- The teacher uses teaching approaches that are sensitive to the multiple experiences of learners and that address different learning and performance modes.
- The teacher makes appropriate provisions (in terms of time and circumstances for work, tasks assigned, communication and response

modes) for individual students who have particular learning differences or needs.

- The teacher can identify when and how to access appropriate services or resources to meet exceptional learning needs.
- The teacher seeks to understand students' families, cultures, and communities, and uses this information as a basis for connecting instruction to students' experiences (e.g., drawing explicit connections between subject matter and community matters, making assignments that can be related to students' experiences and cultures).
- The teacher brings multiple perspectives to the discussion of subject matter, including attention to students' personal, family, and community experiences and cultural norms.
- The teacher creates a learning community in which individual differences are respected.

Principle #4 *The teacher understands and uses a variety of instructional strategies to encourage students' development of critical thinking, problem solving, and performance skills.*

Knowledge

- The teacher understands the cognitive processes associated with various kinds of learning (e.g., critical and creative thinking, problem structuring and problem solving, invention, memorization and recall) and how these processes can be stimulated.
- The teacher understands principles and techniques, along with advantages and limitations, associated with various instructional strategies (e.g., cooperative learning, direct instruction, discovery learning, whole group discussion, independent study, interdisciplinary instruction).
- The teacher knows how to enhance learning through the use of a wide variety of materials as well as human and technological resources (e.g., computers, audiovisual technologies, videotapes and discs, local experts, primary documents and artifacts, texts, reference books, literature, and other print resources).

Dispositions

- The teacher values the development of students' critical thinking, independent problem solving, and performance capabilities.
- The teacher values flexibility and reciprocity in the teaching process as necessary for adapting instruction to student responses, ideas, and needs.

Performances

- The teacher carefully evaluates how to achieve learning goals, choosing alternative teaching strategies and materials to achieve different instructional purposes and to meet student needs (e.g., developmental stages, prior knowledge, learning styles, and interests).

- The teacher uses multiple teaching and learning strategies to engage students in active learning opportunities that promote the development of critical thinking, problem solving, and performance capabilities and that help student assume responsibility for identifying and using learning resources.
- The teacher constantly monitors and adjusts strategies in response to learner feedback.
- The teacher varies his or her role in the instructional process (e.g., instructor, facilitator, coach, audience) in relation to the content and purposes of instruction and the needs of students.
- The teacher develops a variety of clear, accurate presentations and representations of concepts, using alternative explanations to assist students' understanding and presenting diverse perspectives to encourage critical thinking.

Principle #5 *The teacher uses an understanding of individual and group motivation and behavior to create a learning environment that encourages positive social interaction, active engagement in learning, and self-motivation.*

Knowledge

- The teacher can use knowledge about human motivation and behavior drawn from the foundational sciences of psychology, anthropology, and sociology to develop strategies for organizing and supporting individual and group work.
- The teacher understands how social groups function and influence people, and how people influence groups.

The effective teacher knows how to help students work productively and cooperatively in complex social settings.

- The teacher knows how to help people work productively and cooperatively with each other in complex social settings.
- The teacher understands the principles of effective classroom management and can use a range of strategies to promote positive relationships, cooperation, and purposeful learning in the classroom.
- The teacher recognizes factors and situations that are likely to promote or diminish intrinsic motivation, and knows how to help students become self-motivated.

Dispositions

- The teacher takes responsibility for establishing a positive climate in the classroom and participates in maintaining such a climate in the school as whole.
- The teacher understands how participation supports commitment, and is committed to the expression and use of democratic values in the classroom.
- The teacher values the role of students in promoting each other's learning and recognizes the importance of peer relationships in establishing a climate of learning.
- The teacher recognizes the value of intrinsic motivation to students' life-long growth and learning.
- The teacher is committed to the continuous development of individual students' abilities and considers how different motivational strategies are likely to encourage this development for each student.

Performances

- The teacher creates a smoothly functioning learning community in which students assume responsibility for themselves and one another, participate in decision making, work collaboratively and independently, and engage in purposeful learning activities.
- The teacher engages students in individual and cooperative learning activities that help them develop the motivation to achieve by, for example, relating lessons to students' personal interests, allowing students to have choices in their learning, and leading students to ask questions and pursue problems that are meaningful to them.
- The teacher organizes, allocates, and manages the resources of time, space, activities, and attention to provide active and equitable engagement of students in productive tasks.
- The teacher maximizes the amount of class time spent in learning by creating expectations and processes for communication and behavior along with a physical setting conducive to classroom goals.
- The teacher helps the group to develop shared values and expectations for student interactions, academic discussions, and individual and

group responsibility that create a positive classroom climate of openness, mutual respect, support, and inquiry.

- The teacher analyzes the classroom environment and makes decisions and adjustments to enhance social relationships, student motivation and engagement, and productive work.
- The teacher organizes, prepares students for, and monitors independent and group work that allows for full and varied participation of all individuals.

Principle #6 *The teacher uses knowledge of effective verbal, nonverbal, and media communication techniques to foster active inquiry, collaboration, and supportive interaction in the classroom.*

Knowledge

- The teacher understands communication theory, language development, and the role of language in learning.
- The teacher understands how cultural and gender differences can affect communication in the classroom.
- The teacher recognizes the importance of nonverbal as well as verbal communication.
- The teacher knows about and can use effective verbal, nonverbal, and media communication techniques.

Dispositions

- The teacher recognizes the power of language for fostering self-expression, identity development, and learning.
- The teacher values many ways in which people seek to communicate and encourages many modes of communication in the classroom.
- The teacher is a thoughtful and responsive listener.
- The teacher appreciates the cultural dimensions of communication, responds appropriately, and seeks to foster culturally sensitive communication by and among all students in the class.

Performances

- The teacher models effective communication strategies in conveying ideas and information and in asking questions (e.g., monitoring the effects of messages, restating ideas and drawing connections, using visual, aural, and kinesthetic cues, being sensitive to nonverbal cues given and received).
- The teacher supports and expands learner expression in speaking, writing, and other media.
- The teacher knows how to ask questions and stimulate discussion in different ways for particular purposes, for example, probing for learner understanding, helping students articulate their ideas and thinking processes, promoting risk taking and problem solving, facilitating factual

recall, encouraging convergent and divergent thinking, stimulating curiosity, helping students to question.

- The teacher communicates in ways that demonstrate a sensitivity to cultural and gender differences (e.g., appropriate use of eye contact, interpretation of body language and verbal statements, acknowledgment of and responsiveness to different modes of communication and participation).
- The teacher knows how to use a variety of media communication tools, including audio-visual aids and computers, to enrich learning opportunities.

Principle #7 *The teacher plans instruction based upon knowledge of subject matter, students, the community, and curriculum goals.*

Knowledge

- The teacher understands learning theory, subject matter, curriculum development, and student development and knows how to use this knowledge in planning instruction to meet curriculum goals.
- The teacher knows how to take contextual considerations (instructional materials, individual student interests, needs, and aptitudes, and community resources) into account in planning instruction that creates an effective bridge between curriculum goals and students' experiences.
- The teacher knows when and how to adjust plans based on student responses and other contingencies.

Dispositions

- The teacher values both long-term and short-term planning.
- The teacher believes that plans must always be open to adjustment and revision based on student needs and changing circumstances.
- The teacher values planning as a collegial activity.

Performances

- As an individual and a member of a team, the teacher selects and creates learning experiences that are appropriate for curriculum goals, relevant to learners, and based on principles of effective instruction (e.g., those experiences that activate students' prior knowledge, anticipate preconceptions, encourage exploration and problem-solving, and build new skills on those previously acquired).
- The teacher plans for learning opportunities that recognize and address variation in learning styles and performance modes.
- The teacher creates lessons and activities that operate at multiple levels to meet the developmental and individual needs of diverse learners and help each progress.
- The teacher creates short-range and long-term plans that are linked to student needs and performance, and adapts the plans to ensure and capitalize on student progress and motivation.

- The teacher responds to unanticipated sources of input, evaluates plans in relation to short- and long-range goals, and systematically adjusts plans to meet student needs and enhance learning.

Principle #8 *The teacher understands and uses formal and informal assessment strategies to evaluate and ensure the continuous intellectual, social and physical development of the learner.*

Knowledge

- The teacher understands the characteristics, uses, advantages, and limitations of different types of assessments (e.g., criterion-referenced and norm-referenced instruments, traditional standardized and performance-based tests, observation systems, and assessments of student work) for evaluating how students learn, what they know and are able to do, and what kinds of experiences will support their further growth and development.
- The teacher knows how to select, construct, and use assessment strategies and instruments appropriate to the learning outcomes being evaluated and to other diagnostic purposes.
- The teacher understands measurement theory and assessment-related issues, such as validity, reliability, bias, and scoring concerns.

Dispositions

- The teacher values ongoing assessment as essential to the instructional process and recognizes that many different assessment strategies, accurately and systematically used, are necessary for monitoring and promoting student learning.
- The teacher is committed to using assessment to identify student strengths and promote student growth rather than to deny students access to learning opportunities.

Performances

- The teacher appropriately uses a variety of formal and informal assessment techniques (e.g., observation, portfolios of student work, teacher-made tests, performance tasks, projects, student self-assessments, peer assessment, and standardized tests) to enhance her or his knowledge of learners, evaluate students' progress and performances, and modify teaching and learning strategies.
- The teacher solicits and uses information about students' experiences, learning behavior, needs, and progress from parents, other colleagues, and the students themselves.
- The teacher uses assessment strategies to involve learners in self-assessment activities, to help them become aware of their strengths and needs, and to encourage them to set personal goals for learning.
- The teacher evaluates the effect of class activities on both individuals and the class as a whole, collecting information through observation of classroom interactions, questioning, and analysis of student work.

Effective teachers help students become aware of their strengths and encourage them to set personal learning goals.

- The teacher monitors his or her own teaching strategies and behavior in relation to student success, modifying plans and instructional approaches accordingly.
- The teacher maintains useful records of student work and performance and can communicate student progress knowledgeably and responsibly, based on appropriate indicators, to students, parents, and other colleagues.

Principle #9 *The teacher is a reflective practitioner who continually evaluates the effects of his/her choices and actions on others (students, parents, and other professionals in the learning community) and who actively seeks out opportunities to grow professionally.*

Knowledge

- The teacher understands methods of inquiry that provide him/her with a variety of self-assessment and problem-solving strategies for reflecting on his/her practice, its influences on students' growth and learning, and the complex interactions between them.
- The teacher is aware of major areas of research on teaching and of resources available for professional learning (e.g., professional literature, colleagues, professional associations, professional development activities).

Dispositions

- The teacher values critical thinking and self-directed learning as habits of mind.
- The teacher is committed to reflection, assessment, and learning as an ongoing process.
- The teacher is willing to give and receive help.
- The teacher is committed to seeking out, developing, and continually refining practices that address the individual needs of students.
- The teacher recognizes his/her professional responsibility for engaging in and supporting appropriate professional practices for self and colleagues.

Performances

- The teacher uses classroom observation, information about students, and research as sources for evaluating the outcomes of teaching and learning and as a basis for experimenting with, reflecting on, and revising practice.
- The teacher seeks out professional literature, colleagues, and other resources to support his/her own development as a learner and a teacher.
- The teacher draws upon professional colleagues within the school and other professional arenas as supports for reflection, problem-solving and new ideas, actively sharing experiences and seeking and giving feedback.

Principle #10 *The teacher fosters relationships with school colleagues, parents, and agencies in the larger community to support students' learning and well-being.*

Knowledge

- The teacher understands schools as organizations within the larger community context and understands the operations of the relevant aspects of the system(s) within which s/he works.
- The teacher understands how factors in the students' environment outside of school (e.g., family circumstances, community environments, health and economic conditions) may influence students' life and learning.
- The teacher understands and implements laws related to students' rights and teacher responsibilities (e.g., for equal education, appropriate education for handicapped students, confidentiality, privacy, appropriate treatment of students, reporting in situations related to possible child abuse).

Dispositions

- The teacher values and appreciates the importance of all aspects of a child's experience.
- The teacher is concerned about all aspects of a child's well-being (cognitive, emotional, social, and physical), and is alert to signs of difficulties.
- The teacher is willing to consult with other adults regarding the education and well-being of his/her students.

- The teacher respects the privacy of students and confidentiality of information.
- The teacher is willing to work with other professionals to improve the overall learning environment for students.

Performances

- The teacher participates in collegial activities designed to make the entire school a productive learning environment.
- The teacher makes links with the learners' other environments on behalf of students, by consulting with parents, counselors, teachers of other classes and activities within the schools, and professionals in other community agencies.
- The teacher can identify and use community resources to foster student learning.
- The teacher establishes respectful and productive relationships with parents and guardians from diverse home and community situations, and seeks to develop cooperative partnerships in support of student learning and well being.
- The teacher talks with and listens to the student, is sensitive and responsive to clues of distress, investigates situations, and seeks outside help as needed and appropriate to remedy problems.
- The teacher acts as an advocate for students.

The INTASC Standards give educational professionals a powerful base by which to assess their performance. The following checklists are among those methods used to assess the classroom performance of teachers.

Checklists for Teacher Assessment/Evaluation

Below are two examples of checklists used to measure and evaluate how well a teacher is doing his or her job. Monitoring teacher performance is a requirement of local school boards, state boards of education, and many accrediting agencies.

Short Observation Checklist

The type of checklist shown in figure 4.1 is often used by principals, supervisors, and other administrators, as well as by mentoring teachers, to record their observations of teachers and student teachers.

Long Observation Checklist

The type of checklist shown in figure 4.2 is often used by principals, supervisors, and other administrators, as well as by mentoring teachers, to record their observations of teachers and student teachers at the conclusion of a six-week or nine-week reporting period, or at the mid-semester or end-of-semester period for student teachers.

Figure 4.1 Short Observation Form

Name:						
1. Unsatisfactory 2. Needs help 3. Satisfactory 4. Good 5. Excellent N/A = Not applicable or not present in the lesson						
Date of observation	Lesson preparation	Poise/ demeanor	Language usage	Eye contact	Classroom management	Activity oriented
	Interest/ motivation	Questioning strategies	Technology component	Grouping strategies	Materials selection	Lesson rhythm
	Interaction with students	Subject knowledge	Lesson Topic: History Geography Economics Civics			
			Teacher:			
			School:			

Comments:

Figure 4.2 Long Observation Form

Student Teacher / Intern:______________________ Date:__________

Name of School:______________________ Period/Block:__________

Grade Level(s):__________ Location:______________

Lesson Topic: ______________________ Course:__________

Please rate each skill accordingly using the stated scale and placing a mark in the appropriate box.

5 – excellent 4 – good 3 – fair 2 – poor 1 – unsatisfactory NA – not applicable or not observable

CHARACTERISTIC/DOMAIN	5	4	3	2	1	NA
PLANNING						
Specifies learner outcomes in clear, concise objectives						
Plans effectively for instruction						
Includes activity/activities that develop objectives						
Identifies and plans for individual differences						
Identifies materials, other than standard classroom materials, as needed for lesson						
States method(s) of evaluation to measure learner outcomes						
MANAGEMENT						
Maintains an environment conducive to learning						
Organizes available space, materials, and/or equipment to facilitate learning.						
Promotes a positive learning climate						
Maximizes the amount of time available for instruction						
Manages routines and transitions in a timely manner						
Manages and/or adjusts time for activities						
Establishes expectations for learner behavior						
Uses monitoring techniques to facilitate learning						
INSTRUCTION						
Delivers instruction effectively						
Uses technique(s) which develop(s) lesson objective(s)						
Sequences lesson to promote learning						
Uses available teaching material(s) to achieve lesson objective(s)						
Adjusts lesson when appropriate						
Integrates technology into instruction						
Presents appropriate content						
Presents content at a developmentally appropriate level						
Presents accurate subject matter						
Relates relevant examples, unexpected situations, or current events to the content						
Provides opportunities for student involvement in the learning process						
Accommodates individual differences						
Demonstrates ability to communicate effectively with students						
Stimulates and encourages higher-order thinking at appropriate development levels						
Encourages student participation						
Assesses student progress						
Consistently monitors ongoing performance of students						
Uses appropriate and effective assessment techniques						
Provides timely feedback to students						
Produces evidence of student academic growth under his/her instruction						
OTHER						
Submitted lesson plan, copy of materials, and seating chart						
Exhibits a positive attitude toward supervision						
Accepts and profits from constructive criticism						
OVERALL PERFORMANCE						

Strengths observed:

Weaknesses observed:

Suggestions for improvement:

Other comments:

Observer ______________________

Official Title ______________________

SECTION V

The Comprehensive Curriculum and Content Standards

The *comprehensive curriculum*[1] is one way to align instruction with standards, benchmarks, and grade-level expectations with the goal of improving student achievement across a state or a school district. Louisiana is one state whose Department of Education has provided a comprehensive curriculum to every school district within the state. The curriculum is aligned with state content standards, as defined by grade-level expectations (or GLEs, discussed later in this section), and organized into coherent, time-bound units with sample activities and classroom assessments to guide teaching and learning.

A written, aligned curriculum brings academic expectations into sharp focus by describing what instruction will be presented, to whom it will be presented, when it will be presented, and how it will be presented. Without a written curriculum, textbooks often become the de facto curriculum of a school or district. Unfortunately, so much is included in textbooks that they have little ability to focus instruction or to provide the depth needed for good teaching and learning

Advantages of the Comprehensive Curriculum

While the comprehensive curriculum may be used in conjunction with textbooks, it will help teachers limit the topics they address to those the standards define as important. This alignment with standards can focus classroom activities and ensure a depth of coverage that will help students achieve mastery. A comprehensive curriculum is helpful to a teacher because it focuses on what is important to teach.

Aligning Content, Instruction, and Assessment to Standards

Curriculum alignment is more than establishing a scope and sequence of instruction. Aligning the curriculum is the process of ensuring a good match between the state standards—specifically, the GLEs—and the lessons taught in classrooms every day. This process ensures that instructional activities are aligned to standards, that an appropriate amount of time is devoted to the activities, that unnecessary repetitions in the instructional program are removed, that gaps in content are identified, and that classroom assessments are appropriate.

Ensuring Access for All Students

Because the comprehensive curriculum is aligned with standards, benchmarks, and grade-level expectations, it has the potential of increasing student achievement and helping to overcome the possible limitations of socioeconomic status, gender, race, and teacher quality. A pre-condition of a successful educational program is a clear and agreed-upon understanding that instructional content and classroom assessments should reflect the instructional standards. In a school district with a well-aligned curriculum, *all* students have the opportunity and responsibility to master the instructional content.

Organizing Content into Coherent, Time-Bound Units

Simply teaching grade-level expectations is likely to fragment knowledge and skills into bits and pieces, much like a collection of puzzle pieces that don't mean anything taken alone. Units of instruction create coherent curriculum contexts that organize and connect learning experiences. A comprehensive curriculum is organized into units that bring together groups of GLEs that make sense as a whole, thus helping students get the "big picture" (like putting all the puzzle pieces together).

Each unit of a comprehensive curriculum should include time frames for mastering grade-level expectations included in the unit. The time frames can help to govern time distribution among the competing subject matter and topics. When curriculum appropriately governs time *and* content, the academic learning time (time spent "on task") increases, and so, then, will student achievement.

Creating Feedback Systems

The units in a comprehensive curriculum include assessment components that strengthen curriculum by providing feedback which indicates whether students have learned what was taught. Many activities in a comprehensive curriculum may be designed to have products, and these products can be assessed using a rubric to determine whether the products indicate mastery by the students.

Principles of Social Studies Teaching and Learning

The National Council for the Social Studies, in recognition of the fact that "the United States and its democracy are constantly evolving and in continuous need of citizens who can adapt its enduring traditions and values to meet changing circumstance," adopted the following formal definition:

> Social studies is the integrated study of the social sciences and humanities to promote civic competence. Within the school program, social studies provides coordinated, systematic study drawing upon such disciplines as anthropology, archaeology, economics, geography, history, law, philosophy, political science, psychology, religion, and sociology, as well as appropriate content from the humanities, mathematics and natural sciences. The primary purpose of social studies is to help young people develop the ability to make informed and reasoned decisions for the public good as citizens of a culturally diverse, democratic society in an interdependent world. (NCSS, 1992)

The challenge for educators is to deliver a curriculum at the local level that will prepare students to be informed, humane, rational, and participating citizens in a world that is interdependent, diverse, economically integrated, and increasingly technological. Effective social studies instruction reinforces democratic principles and ideals of citizenship. A solid base of social studies knowledge and skills develops civic competence by focusing on rights, responsibilities, and respect.

As citizens of a democracy, we, as social studies educators, support one of our republic's most important ideals: the common good—the general welfare of all individuals and groups within the community. Social studies instruction ideally promotes respect for and the dignity of the individual, the health of the community, and the common good of all.

Skills and Content

As discussed in Section II, a foundation of four core disciplines, or strands, from the social sciences—*geography, civics, economics,* and *history*—are generally used to develop content standards in most high schools because of their course offerings. Within these core strands, sociology, anthropology, psychology, and other "subdisciplines" are incorporated where appropriate. An additional component often included is the foundational skills associated with all disciplines: communication, problem solving, resource access and utilization, linking and generating knowledge, and citizenship (see Section II). These strands and foundation skills, along with grade-level expectations, help to define scope and sequence and assist in the development of appropriate tools for assessing student learning.

Each discipline in social studies demands certain skills in order for students to engage in meaningful learning of content—for example, historical thinking skills. Meaningful historical understanding requires students to engage in five categories of historical thinking. These include (1) developing a sense of historical time and historical perspective, (2) explaining and analyzing historical events and ideas, (3) interpreting and evaluating historical evidence in primary and secondary sources, (4) using historical inquiry to analyze historical and contemporary issues and conduct historical research, and (5) analyzing cause-effect relationships. These skills are not mutually exclusive in an instructional setting, nor do they prescribe a particular teaching sequence. While historical thinking skills can be described absent of historical content, they cannot be developed or practiced in a vacuum.

Instructional Practice

Some learning cannot be packaged easily, and as educators we struggle every day to find the right formula. For social studies in particular, there is a built-in dilemma. It is one discipline in the school where no human knowledge is off limits and where the ability to bring any and all relevant information to a human problem makes the discipline unique and dynamic. Because of these complex factors, the discipline cannot be neatly and easily defined, packaged, and presented by a logical, sequential formula; therefore, it is helpful to have an aligned curriculum.

Strategies

Achieving a meaningful level of depth in social studies instruction requires focus. Social studies content provides numerous opportunities for teachers to expand student understanding of their country and the world. Necessary parameters for content focus are provided by grade-level expectations, but the grade-level expectations should not limit the types of strategies and activities that make social studies meaningful to students. Within the parameters of the expectations, allowing students to choose the topics they explore actually helps them practice their rights and responsibilities as school citizens.

To make their studies relevant, and to support their growth as community citizens, students can be encouraged to practice problem solving and inquiry through participating in local organizations—social, political, and economic. Such activities can be planned to integrate several content areas. For example, the cleanup of a park might involve organizing other students and community members, investigating plant and animal life, and calculating the relative costs of landfills and recycling for trash found on the site. In addition, exploring the cultural diversity of their community can help students understand their place in their world.

Materials

Meaningful social studies instruction requires an array of materials to provide adequate instructional support. While a textbook may be a reasonable bottom-line resource, class sets of original documents, journal articles, appropriate maps, newspapers, news magazines, and other historical and current materials help students to explore and discuss past and present issues. In addition, teachers need ready access to the world of information—and they must understand how to integrate the information into daily activities. Internet connections, as well as other visual and audio technologies, need to be readily available to the social studies classroom. Lack of access to an array of nontext materials restricts teachers' abilities to deliver the kind of active instruction envisioned in a comprehensive curriculum.

Instructional Technology

A quality social studies program ensures that each student has access to necessary technological tools and can use these tools to implement the curriculum. The opportunities afforded by computer networking and the Internet are exciting for teachers and students, because these technologies enable them to access information—and provide them with teaching and learning tools—that may not be available in an alternate format.

A quality social studies program ensures that each student has access to necessary technological tools and can use these tools to implement the curriculum.

Internet resources can provide teachers and students with information on a wide array of topics and issues. Online educational partners can benefit learners by supplying primary sources; interactive maps, trips, and tours; and other classroom resources. In addition, the Internet provides opportunities for students to learn from their peers across the United States and the world via digital technologies, cooperative Web sites, and programs that link schools on topics of interest.

Used in conjunction with instructional software that provides engaging simulations and databases that enable students to manipulate information, the tools of the Information Age can help students relive history and conduct authentic social studies research.

Cross-Curricular Connections

Social studies is an interdisciplinary and multidisciplinary field of study. While social studies standards and grade-level expectations define the core learning, social studies instruction makes use of understandings from all content areas. This interdisciplinary curriculum connects to the real world by providing students with an expanded understanding of the interconnected nature of the world through an integrated approach that provides focus and depth.

Components of a Comprehensive Curriculum

The components of a comprehensive curriculum are intended to be reflective of the components that should be included in any good curriculum. The components that would be typical of a comprehensive curriculum are described in table 5.1.

The unit-organizer format allows teachers to see the interrelationships among the grade-level expectations and indicates "best practice" activities that should be used when teaching a particular concept or skill. Table 5.2 explains the elements in a comprehensive curriculum unit.

The elements of the comprehensive curriculum are set forth using standards, benchmarks, and GLEs. These are discussed in the following section.

Table 5.1 Components of a Comprehensive Curriculum

Curriculum Component	Explanation
Cover page/title page	Displays content area and courses included in the document, name of the agency that developed the document, and the date the document was developed
Board of Education	Lists the names of board members who approved the use of the curriculum document and the name of the superintendent
Acknowledgments (optional)	Lists individuals or groups who contributed to the development of the local curriculum
Table of contents	Lists the courses and other curriculum components and where they can be found in the document
Preface	Provides background information including underlying law and policies that led to the development of the document
Purpose	Provides a statement of the intended purpose of the written, aligned curriculum, expectations for its use in the classroom, and the expected results in terms of student performance
Principles of teaching and learning for specific content area	States beliefs about the content area and research-based principles of successful teaching and learning
Professional development	Provides a summary statement of how appropriate professional development ensures that teachers possess knowledge and skills needed to teach the new curriculum
Pre-K–12 courses	Includes a copy of each course in the relevant content area

Table 5.2 Comprehensive Curriculum Unit

Unit Element	Explanation
Time frame	Each unit of instruction has a specific time frame (e.g., approximately two to three weeks). The time frame helps teachers pace instruction and learning. The time frame also helps administrators monitor the implementation of the curriculum.
Course name	Specifies the grade level and the content area for courses pre-kindergarten through grade 8 (e.g., grade 3 English Language Arts). For high school courses (grades 9–12), the name specifies the content (e.g., U.S. History).
Unit title	Each unit has a title designed to sharpen focus on the collection of ideas and concepts to be learned in that unit (e.g., poetry, measuring and comparing).
Unit number	Units are numbered sequentially (Unit 1, Unit 2, etc.).
Unit description	States broadly, in one or two sentences, the intent of the unit (e.g., The focus of this unit is how the availability of resources influences economic decisions).
Student understandings	A brief description of the overarching concepts to be learned by the student.
Guiding questions	A list of questions that teachers can use to determine if students understand the concepts being taught (e.g., Can students use the structure of the article to find information they need?)
Grade-level expectations (GLEs)	Each unit has a table that lists the number and the text of each GLE to be addressed by the unit. Benchmark codes are included at the end of each GLE.
Sample activities	Each activity is numbered, named, and lists the GLE(s) that are addressed by the activity, providing guidance to teachers as they plan their lessons throughout the school year.
Sample assessments	At the end of each unit are suggested assessments that are linked to the processes of teaching and learning (e.g., graded homework, class projects, performance tasks, discussions with teachers/parents/classmates, diagnostic tests, teacher-made tests and quizzes, observation systems, performance assessment based on performance levels as defined by rubrics, portfolios, and so on).

Standards, Benchmarks, and Grade-Level Expectations

- *Grade-level expectations* (GLEs) are statements that define *what all students should know and be able to do at the end of a given grade level*. GLEs add further definition to the content standards and benchmarks.

- *Content standards* are *broad statements* that represent the *overarching goals* that describe what students should know and be able to do.
- *Benchmarks* are more specific statements of what all students should know and be able to do that are written for specific grade clusters.

Understanding Grade-Level Expectations

Grade-level expectations are directly related to benchmarks and define what the benchmark means for a given grade. Each grade-level expectation is meant to further define a content standard and benchmark(s). There is a progression of specificity; the standards represent broad statements, benchmarks are more specific, and GLEs provide the most detail.

GLEs do not represent the entire curriculum for a given grade or course. Rather, they represent the core content that should be mastered by the end of a given year by all students. For mastery to be achieved at a given level, it may be necessary for those skills to be introduced at an earlier grade. Similarly, skills will need to be maintained after mastery has occurred. GLEs help articulate learning from pre-K through grade 12, are appropriate to the developmental levels of students, move from the concrete to the abstract, and give attention to prerequisite skills and understandings. The GLEs for each grade are developmentally appropriate, with foundational concepts being introduced in pre-kindergarten and expanded as students move from one grade to the next.

Grade-level expectations for social studies further define the knowledge and skills students are expected to master by the end of each grade level or high school course. Social studies concepts are arranged to build the knowledge and skills students will need to meet the benchmarks. For example, the foundation needed to achieve the K–4 benchmark, "demonstrating how economic wants affect decisions about using goods and services," is laid beginning in Pre-K with the GLE, "demonstrate an awareness of the uses of money in play activities." In each subsequent elementary grade, there are GLEs that build on this foundational economic concept. Knowledge and skills related to economic decisions continue to build in middle school. In high school, students are then expected to "identify factors that drive economic decisions (e.g., incentives, benefits, costs, trade-offs, consequences)."

In addition to the goal of building knowledge and skills across the grades, the GLEs are organized so that each elementary and middle school grade has a particular focus. High school GLEs are organized around core content courses.

Each middle school grade also has a secondary focus. In fifth and sixth grades, the secondary focus is Geography. At these grades, students continue to broaden their perspective of the world through the study of Geography and to develop the geographic concepts that will be applied in the study of History at succeeding grades. In seventh grade, the secondary focus is Civics, as early U.S. History provides a rich context for the study of government. The secondary focus for eighth grade is Economics, in part because many of the economic concepts in the benchmarks are more developmentally appropriate for eighth graders than for younger students.

It is important to note that while each grade has a primary and a secondary focus, students are expected to apply their knowledge and skills from other strands in their study of History. For example, previously mastered economic concepts, such as scarcity and interdependence, are embedded in seventh-grade U.S. History GLEs that address the issues of mercantilism, tariffs, and sectionalism. Similarly, Geography skills mastered at fifth and sixth grades are reinforced and applied at all succeeding grades.

High School GLEs (Grades 9–12). The GLEs for high school are developed around five core courses in high school social studies to provide students more in-depth study of each social studies strand: Geography (core course: World Geography), Civics (core course: Civics), Economics (core course: Free Enterprise); and History (core courses: World History–since 1500 and U.S. History–since 1877). Students are expected to build on the knowledge and skills mastered at earlier grades in order to meet the high school GLEs and benchmarks. For example, in the U.S. History–since 1877 course, students use what they learned in seventh-grade U.S. History as a basis for their understanding and analysis of later history. Additionally, students' foundational knowledge and skills in geography, civics, and economics are applied in the U.S. History GLEs.

Historical Thinking Skills. A set of unifying GLEs related to historical thinking skills (substrand A of the History strand) are present in every grade from pre-kindergarten through eighth grade, and in the two high school History courses. These historical thinking skills build throughout the grades, asking students to progress from concrete skills (e.g., understanding relative chronology) to complex analytical skills (e.g., analyzing historical periods, change, and continuity). These skills are embedded and applied meaningfully throughout the study of social studies and are not mastered in isolation.

Linking Benchmarks and GLEs

Codes at the end of each GLE are used to identify a developmental profile indicator from the benchmarks in the table below. A GLE may apply to more than one benchmark, and as a result a GLE may have more than one code.

Benchmark Codes. Benchmark codes have three parts. The first part identifies the strand (i.e., geography, civics, economics, or history). The second part gives the standard number and substrand. The third part indicates the grade cluster and benchmark number (see table 5.3). The foundational skills (discussed in Section II of this book) are listed numerically at the end of each benchmark.

Table 5.3 Explanation of Benchmark Codes

Code(s)	Explanation
G-1A-E1	Geography, Standard 1, Substrand A, Elementary Benchmark 1
C-1B-E2	Civics, Standard 1, Substrand B, Elementary School, Benchmark 2
E-1C-M2	Economics, Standard 1, Substrand C, Middle School, Benchmark 2
H-1C-H3	History, Standard 1, Substrand C, High School, Benchmark 3

STANDARDS AND BENCHMARKS FOR TEACHING WORLD HISTORY

(Usually an elective or alternate to world geography)

HISTORY: Time, Continuity, and Change

FOCUS: History, the written record of the past, examines the forces of change and continuity that have influenced the human experience over time. In our participatory democracy, that knowledge must be shared by all. Americans need to understand the relationships between past and present, the major trends in the historic and contemporary worlds, and key historical turning points. The study of the great sweep of history explains the past so that citizens can understand the present and look toward the future. The standards and benchmarks contained in this strand should be applied throughout the social studies curriculum.

STANDARD: Students develop a sense of historical time and historical perspective as they study the history of their community, state, nation, and world.

BENCHMARKS 9–12: As students in grades 9–12 extend and refine their knowledge, what they know and are able to do includes:

Historical Thinking Skills

H-1A-H1 applying key concepts, such as chronology and conflict, to explain and analyze patterns of historical change and continuity; (1, 2, 3, 4)

H-1A-H2 explaining and analyzing events, ideas, and issues within a historical context; (1, 2, 3, 4)

H-1A-H3 interpreting and evaluating the historical evidence presented in primary and secondary sources; (1, 2, 3, 4)

H-1A-H4 utilizing knowledge of facts and concepts drawn from history and methods of historical inquiry to analyze historical and contemporary issues; (1, 2, 3, 4, 5)

H-1A-H5 conducting research in efforts to analyze historical questions and issues; (1, 2, 3, 4)

H-1A-H6 analyzing cause-effect relationships; (1, 2, 3, 4)

The Beginnings of Society

H-1C-H1 analyzing the development of early human communities and civilizations; (1, 2, 3, 4)

The Rise of Early Civilizations (4000–1000 BC)

H-1C-H2 making generalizations about the cultural legacies of both the ancient river and the classical civilizations; (1, 3, 4)

Classical Traditions, Major Religions, and Giant Empire (1000 BC–AD 300)

H-1C-H3 analyzing the origins, central ideas, and worldwide impact of major religious and philosophical traditions; (1, 2, 3, 4)

Expanding Zones of Exchange and Encounter (AD 300–1000)

H-1C-H4 summarizing the developments and contributions of civilizations that flourished in Europe, Asia, Africa, and the Americas; (1, 3, 4)

Intensified Hemispheric Interactions (AD 1000–1500)

H-1C-H5 analyzing the consequences of the economic and cultural interchange that increasingly developed among the peoples of Europe, Asia, and Africa; (1, 2, 3, 4)

Emergence of the First Global Age (1450–1770)

H-1C-H6 analyzing the impact of transoceanic linking of all major regions of the world; (1, 2, 3, 4)

H-1C-H7 analyzing the political, cultural, and economic developments and trends that resulted in the transformation of major world regions; (1, 2, 3, 4)

H-1C-H8 explaining how the emergence of territorial empires in Europe, Asia, and Africa unified large areas politically, economically, and culturally; (1, 3, 4)

H-1C-H9 tracing the expansion of European power and economic influence in the world and examining the impact of this expansion on societies in Asia and the Americas; (1, 3, 4)

An Age of Revolutions (1750–1914)

H-1C-H10 analyzing the impact that political revolutions and new ideologies had on societies around the world; (1, 2, 3, 4)

H-1C-H11 evaluating the economic, political, and social consequences of the agricultural and industrial revolutions on world societies; (1, 2, 3, 4)

H-1C-H12 analyzing the patterns of worldwide change that emerged during the era of Western military and economic domination; (1, 2, 3, 4)

A Half-Century of Crisis and Achievement (1900–1945)

H-1C-H13 analyzing the causes and international consequences of World War I, the rise and actions of totalitarian systems, World War II, and other early twentieth-century conflicts; (1, 2, 3, 4)

The 20th Century Since 1945 (1945–1999)

H-1C-H14 analyzing the international power shifts and the breakup of colonial empires that occurred in the years following World War II; (1, 2, 3, 4)

H-1C-H15 explaining the worldwide significance of major political, economic, social, cultural, and technological developments and trends. (1, 2, 3, 4, 5)

Grade-Level Expectations for Teaching World History

(Usually an elective or alternate to world geography)

For the high school World History course, the grade-level expectations begin with a focus on the period of exploration and expansion and conclude with contemporary world trends and issues. Students use what they learned in grade 6 (World History to 1500) as a starting point for their study, understanding, and analysis of later history. The foundational historical thinking skills learned in earlier grades are still applied, but with an increased emphasis on analysis and evaluation in addressing major historical topics in the modern world. Students are also expected to apply their knowledge and skills in Economics, Civics, and Geography in the study of World History and contemporary issues.

Historical Thinking Skills

1. Construct a time line to explain and analyze historical periods in world history (H-1A-H1)
2. Compare historical periods or historical conflicts in terms of similar issues, actions, or trends in world history (H-1A-H1)
3. Contrast past and present events or ideas in world history, demonstrating awareness of differing political, social, or economic context (H-1A-H1)
4. Analyze change or continuity in areas of the world over time based on information in stimulus material (H-1A-H1)
5. Describe multiple perspectives on an historical issue or event in world history (H-1A-H2)
6. Analyze the point of view of an historical figure or group in world history (H-1A-H2)
7. Analyze or interpret a given historical event, idea, or issue in world history (H-1A-H2)
8. Debate a historical point of view, with supporting evidence, on an issue or event in world history (H-1A-H2)
9. Evaluate and use multiple primary or secondary materials to interpret historical facts, ideas, or issues (H-1A-H3)
10. Determine when primary and/or secondary sources would be most useful when analyzing historical events (H-1A-H3)
11. Propose and defend alternative courses of action to address an historical or contemporary issue, and evaluate their positive and negative implications (H-1A-H4)
12. Analyze and evaluate the credibility of a given historical document (e.g., in terms of its source, unstated assumptions) (H-1A-H4)
13. Analyze source material to identify opinion or propaganda and persuasive techniques (H-1A-H4)
14. Interpret a political cartoon depicting an historical event, issue, or perspective (H-1A-H4)
15. Interpret or analyze historical data in a map, table, or graph to explain historical factors or trends (H-1A-H4)
16. Construct a narrative summary of an historical speech or address (H-1A-H5)
17. Conduct historical research using a variety of resources to answer historical questions related to world history and present that research in appropriate format(s) (visual, electronic, written) (H-1A-H5)
18. Analyze causes and effects in historical and contemporary world events, using a variety of resources (H-1A-H6)

19. Explain the origins, developments, and consequences of the transatlantic slave trade between Africa and the Americas and Europe (H-1C-H6)
20. Identify major technological innovations in shipbuilding, navigation, and naval warfare, and explain how these technological advances were related to European voyages of exploration, conquest, and colonization (H-1C-H6)
21. Identify demographic, economic, and social trends in major world regions (H-1C-H7)
22. Describe key features of the Renaissance, Reformation, Scientific Revolution, and the Age of Enlightenment (H-1C-H7)
23. Describe major changes in world political boundaries between 1450 and 1770 and assess the extent and limitations of European political and military power in Africa, Asia, and the Americas as of the mid-eighteenth century (H-1C-H8)
24. Describe the development of nation-states and major world powers (H-1C-H8)
25. Describe the goals and consequences of European colonization in the Americas (H-1C-H9)
26. Describe the European commercial penetration of Asia and the impact on trade (H-1C-H9)
27. Identify the influence of European economic power within Africa and its impact on other parts of the world (H-1C-H9)
28. Describe the major ideas of philosophers and their effects on the world (H-1C-H10)
29. Identify causes and evaluate effects of major political revolutions since the seventeenth century (H-1C-H10)
30. Describe how the American Revolution differed from the French Revolution and the impact both had on world political developments (H-1C-H10)
31. Describe the characteristics of the agricultural revolution that occurred in England and Western Europe and analyze its effects on population growth, industrialization, and patterns of landholding (H-1C-H11)
32. Describe the expansion of industrial economies and the resulting social transformations throughout the world (e.g., urbanization, change in daily work life) (H-1C-H11)
33. Describe the motives, major events, and effects of Western European and American imperialism in Africa, Asia, and the Americas (H-1C-H12)
34. Using a map, identify the extent of European and American territorial expansion (H-1C-H12)

Standards and Benchmarks for Teaching American History

(Recommended for Eleventh Grade)

History: Time, Continuity, and Change

Focus: History, the written record of the past, examines the forces of change and continuity that have influenced the human experience over time. In our participatory democracy, that knowledge must be shared by all. Americans need to understand the relationships between past and present, the major trends in the historic and contemporary worlds, and key historical turning points. The study of the great sweep of history explains the past so that citizens can understand the present and look toward the future. The standards and benchmarks contained in this strand should be applied throughout the social studies curriculum.

STANDARD: Students develop a sense of historical time and historical perspective as they study the history of their community, state, nation, and world.

BENCHMARKS 9–12: As students in grades 9–12 extend and refine their knowledge, what they know and are able to do includes:

Historical Thinking Skills

H-1A-H1 applying key concepts, such as chronology and conflict, to explain and analyze patterns of historical change and continuity; (1, 2, 3, 4)

H-1A-H2 explaining and analyzing events, ideas, and issues within a historical context; (1, 2, 3, 4)

H-1A-H3 interpreting and evaluating the historical evidence presented in primary and secondary sources; (1, 2, 3, 4)

H-1A-H4 utilizing knowledge of facts and concepts drawn from history and methods of historical inquiry to analyze historical and contemporary issues; (1, 2, 3, 4, 5)

H-1A-H5 conducting research in efforts to analyze historical questions and issues; (1, 2, 3, 4)

H-1A-H6 analyzing cause-effect relationships; (1, 2, 3, 4)

Three Worlds Meet (Beginnings to 1620)

H-1B-H1 analyzing the significant changes that resulted from interactions among the peoples of Europe, Africa, and the Americas; (1, 2, 3, 4)

Colonization and Settlement (1565–1763)

H-1B-H2 summarizing the process by which the United States was colonized and later became an independent nation; (1, 4)

Revolution and the New Nation (1754–1820s)

H-1B-H3 analyzing the development of the American constitutional system; (1, 2, 3, 4)

Expansion and Reform (1801–1861)

H-1B-H4 tracing territorial expansion and reform movements in the United States; (1, 3, 4)

Civil War and Reconstruction (1850–1877)

H-1B-H5 analyzing the origins, major events, and effects of the Civil War and Reconstruction; (1, 2, 3, 4)

The Development of the Industrial United States (1870–1900)

H-1B-H6 analyzing the development of industrialization and examining its impact on American society; (1, 2, 3, 4)

H-1B-H7 describing the immigration and internal migration patterns that have occurred in the history of the United States and examining the cultural and social changes that have resulted; (1, 2, 3, 4)

The Emergence of Modern America (1890–1930)

H-1B-H8 evaluating the significance of the Progressive Movement; (1, 2, 3, 4)

H-1B-H9 analyzing the rise of the labor and agrarian movements; (1, 2, 3, 4)

H-1B-H10 explaining the changing role of the United States in world affairs through World War I; (1, 3, 4)

H-1B-H11 analyzing the significant changes that evolved in the United States between World War I and the Great Depression; (1, 2, 3, 4)

The Great Depression and World War II (1929–1945)

H-1B-H12 analyzing the causes, developments, and effects of the Great Depression and the New Deal; (1, 2, 3, 4)

H-1B-H13 analyzing the origins, course, and results of World War II; (1, 2, 3, 4)

Contemporary United States (1945 to the Present)

H-1B-H14 examining and summarizing key developments and issues in foreign and domestic policies during the Cold War era; (1, 2, 3, 4)

H-1B-H15 analyzing the economic, political, social, and cultural transformation of the United States since World War II; (1, 2, 3, 4, 5)

H-1B-H16 explaining the major changes that have resulted as the United States has moved from an industrial to an information society; (1, 3, 4)

H-1B-H17 analyzing developments and issues in contemporary American society; (1, 2, 3, 4, 5)

H-1B-H18 discussing and demonstrating an understanding of recent developments in foreign and domestic policies. (1, 2, 3, 4, 5)

Grade-Level Expectations for Teaching American History

(Recommended for Eleventh Grade)

In the high school U.S. History course, the grade-level expectations begin with a focus on late nineteenth-century industrialization and urbanization of America and conclude with a focus on contemporary issues and challenges in the United States. Students use what they learned in grade 7 (U.S. History to 1877) as a basis for their study, understanding, and analysis of later history. The foundational historical thinking skills learned in earlier grades are still applied but with an increased emphasis on analysis and evaluation in addressing major historical topics in modern U.S. History. Students are also expected to apply their knowledge and skills in Economics, Civics, and Geography in the study of U.S. History.

Historical Thinking Skills

1. Construct a time line to explain and analyze historical periods in U.S. history (H-1A-H1)
2. Compare historical periods or historical conflicts in terms of similar issues, actions, or trends in U.S. history (H-1A-H1)
3. Contrast past and present events or ideas in U.S. history, demonstrating awareness of differing political, social, or economic context (H-1A-H1)
4. Analyze change or continuity in the United States over time based on information in stimulus material (H-1A-H1)

5. Describe multiple perspectives on an historical issue or event in U.S. history (H-1A-H2)
6. Analyze the point of view of an historical figure or group in U.S. history (H-1A-H2)
7. Analyze or interpret a given historical event, idea, or issue in U.S. history (H-1A-H2)
8. Debate an historical point of view, with supporting evidence, on an issue or event in U.S. history (H-1A-H2)
9. Evaluate and use multiple primary or secondary materials to interpret historical facts, ideas, or issues (H-1A-H3)
10. Determine when primary and/or secondary sources would be most useful when analyzing historical events (H-1A-H3)
11. Propose and defend alternative courses of action to address an historical or contemporary issue, and evaluate their positive and negative implications (H-1A-H4)
12. Analyze and evaluate the credibility of a given historical document (e.g., in terms of its source, unstated assumptions) (H-1A-H4)
13. Analyze source material to identify opinion or propaganda and persuasive techniques (H-1A-H4)
14. Interpret a political cartoon depicting an historical event, issue, or perspective (H-1A-H4)
15. Interpret or analyze historical data in a map, table, or graph to explain historical factors or trends (H-1A-H4)
16. Construct a narrative summary of an historical speech or address (H-1A-H5)
17. Conduct historical research using a variety of resources to answer historical questions related to U.S. history and present that research in appropriate format(s) (visual, electronic, written) (H-1A-H5)
18. Analyze causes and effects in historical and contemporary U.S. events, using a variety of resources (H-1A-H6)
19. Examine the causes of industrialization and analyze its impact on production, business structures, the work force, and society in the United States (H-1B-H6)
20. Describe the emergence of big business and analyze how it changed American society in the late nineteenth century (H-1B-H6)
21. Analyze the changing relationship between the federal government and private industry (H-1B-H6)
22. Describe the phases, geographic origins, and motivations behind mass migration to and within the United States (H-1B-H7)
23. Explain the causes of the late nineteenth-century urbanization of the United States, including immigration and migration from rural areas, and discuss its impact in such areas as housing, political structures, and public health (H-1B-H7)
24. Explain the impact of legislation, federal Indian and land policies, technological developments, and economic policies on established social and migratory groups in the settlement of the western United States (e.g., Dawes Act, Chinese Exclusion Act) (H-1B-H7)

25. Analyze the role of the media, political leaders, and intellectuals in raising awareness of social problems among Americans in the United States (e.g., Muckrakers, Presidents Roosevelt, Taft, and Wilson, Jane Adams) (H-1B-H8)
26. Evaluate the Progressive Movement in terms of its goals and resulting accomplishments (e.g., Sixteenth through Nineteenth Amendments, Pure Food and Drug Act, advances in land conservation) (H-1B-H8)
27. Describe problems facing farmers and laborers, the ways they sought to enact change, and the responses of the government and business community (e.g., populism, sharecroppers, rise of labor unions) (H-1B-H9)
28. Locate on a world map the territories acquired by the United States during its emergence as an imperial power in the world and explain how these territories were acquired (H-1B-H10)
29. Explain the U.S. policy of imperialism and how it increased U.S. involvement in world affairs (H-1B-H10)
30. Identify causes of World War I (H-1B-H10)
31. Describe the events that led to U.S. involvement in World War I (H-1B-H10)
32. Identify and describe significant events and issues during World War I (H-1B-H10)
33. Identify and explain the consequences of World War I, in terms of changes in U.S foreign and domestic policies during the 1920s (e.g., Treaty of Versailles, Wilson's Fourteen Points, League of Nations) (H-1B-H11)
34. Identify the characteristics of the 1920s and describe the cultural changes that resulted (e.g., Harlem Renaissance, prohibition, women's suffrage) (H-1B-H11)
35. Analyze the international and domestic events, interests, and philosophies that prompted threats to civil liberties in the aftermath of World War I (H-1B-H11)
36. Identify the causes of the Great Depression (e.g., overspeculation, Stock Market Crash of 1929) and analyze its impact on American society (H-1B-H12)
37. Explain the expanding role of government as a result of the Great Depression and the New Deal and analyze the effects of the New Deal legislation (H-1B-H12)
38. Describe the conditions that led to the outbreak of World War II (H-1B-H13)
39. Describe the events that led the United States into World War II (H-1B-H13)
40. Describe the course of World War II, including major turning points and key strategic decisions (H-1B-H13)
41. Describe the effects of World War II on the U.S. home front and Europe, including the Holocaust (H-1B-H13)
42. Explain the consequences and impact of World War II (e.g., Cold War, United Nations, Baby Boom) (H-1B-H13)
43. Analyze the spread of Communism after World War II and its impact on U.S. foreign policy (H-1B-H14)
44. Analyze the conflicts that resulted from Cold War tensions (e.g., Vietnam War, Korean War) (H-1B-H14)
45. Describe the impact of the Cold War on American society and domestic policy (e.g., McCarthyism, Space Race) (H-1B-H14)

46. Analyze the reasons for the end of the Cold War and its impact on the world today (H-1B-H14)
47. Explain the impact of post-World War II domestic policies on life in the United States (e.g., the Great Society) (H-1B-H15)
48. Identify the primary leaders of the Civil Rights Movement and describe major issues and accomplishments (H-1B-H15)
49. Describe the effects of Watergate on the United States and its political system (H-1B-H15)
50. Identify and describe the social and cultural changes from the 1960s to the present (e.g., Women's Movement) (H-1B-H15)
51. Evaluate various means of achieving equality of political rights (e.g., civil disobedience vs. violent protest) (H-1B-H15)
52. Evaluate the effects of the mass media on American society (H-1B-H16)
53. Describe the impact of technology on American society (H-1B-H16)
54. Analyze contemporary issues in American society and suggest alternative solutions (H-1B-H17)
55. Identify recent U.S. Supreme Court decisions and describe how they impact political and social institutions (e.g., presidential election of 2000) (H-1B-H17)
56. Describe the relationship of the United States and nations of the world in the post-Cold War era (e.g., Middle East conflicts, U.S. peacekeeping) (H-1B-H18)
57. Identify recent trends in the U.S. economy and explain shifts in government policy designed to address them (e.g., NAFTA, global economy) (H-1B-H18)
58. Identify and explain recent domestic issues and reform movements (e.g., terrorism, energy, environment, war on drugs, education) (H-1B-H18)

Standards and Benchmarks for Teaching World Geography

(Recommended for Ninth Grade)

Geography: Physical and Cultural Systems

Focus: Geography, the study of the spatial aspects of human existence, enables students to find answers to questions about the world around them. A geographically informed person sees, understands, and appreciates the connections among people, places, and environments. Understanding these connections requires an acute awareness of space, which can be identified in terms of location, distance, direction, pattern, shape, and arrangement. With a strong grasp of geography, students will be prepared to understand issues and solve problems in the contemporary world. The standards and benchmarks contained in this strand should be applied throughout the social studies curriculum.

Standard: Students develop a spatial understanding of Earth's surface and the processes that shape it, the connections between people and places, and the relationship between man and his environment.

Benchmarks 9–12: As students in Grades 9–12 extend and refine their knowledge, what they know and are able to do includes:

The World in Spatial Terms

G-1A-H1 using geographic representations, tools, and technologies to explain, analyze, and solve geographic problems; (1, 2, 3, 4)

G-1A-H2 organizing geographic information and answering complex questions by formulating mental maps of places and regions; (1, 2, 3, 4)

Places and Regions

G-1B-H1 determining how location and social, cultural, and economic processes affect the features and significance of places; (1, 2, 3, 4)

G-1B-H2 analyzing the ways in which physical and human characteristics of places and regions have affected historic events; (1, 2, 3, 4)

G-1B-H3 analyzing the various ways in which physical and human regions are structured and interconnected; (1, 2, 3, 4)

G-1B-H4 explaining and evaluating the importance of places and regions to cultural identity; (1, 2, 3, 4, 5)

Physical and Human Systems

G-1C-H1 analyzing the ways in which Earth's dynamic and interactive physical processes affect different regions of the world; (1, 2, 3, 4)

G-1C-H2 determining the economic, political, and social factors that contribute to human migration and settlement patterns and evaluating their impact on physical and human systems; (1, 2, 3, 4)

G-1C-H3 analyzing trends in world population numbers and patterns and predicting their consequences; (1, 2, 3, 4)

G-1C-H4 analyzing the characteristics, distribution, and interrelationships of the world's cultures; (1, 2, 3, 4, 5)

G-1C-H5 describing and evaluating spatial distribution of economic systems and how economic systems affect regions; (1, 3)

G-1C-H6 analyzing how cooperation, conflict, and self-interests impact social, political, and economic entities on Earth; (1, 2, 3, 4, 5)

Environment and Society

G-1D-H1 describing and evaluating the ways in which technology has expanded the human capability to modify the physical environment; (1, 2, 3, 4, 5)

G-1D-H2 examining the challenges placed on human systems by the physical environment and formulating strategies to deal with these challenges; (1, 2, 3, 4, 5)

G-1D-H3 analyzing the relationship between natural resources and the exploration, colonization, settlement, and uses of land in different regions of the world; (1, 2, 3, 4, 5)

G-1D-H4 evaluating policies and programs related to the use of natural resources; (1, 2, 3, 4, 5)

G-1D-H5 developing plans to solve local and regional geographic problems related to contemporary issues. (1, 2, 3, 4, 5)

Grade-Level Expectations for Teaching World Geography

(Recommended for Ninth Grade)

For the high school World Geography course, the grade-level expectations reflect the use of the Five Themes of Geography to study geographic ideas and concepts. Students are expected to use geographic perspective and spatial tools to study physical and human systems, places and regions, and human and environment interaction. Students also study geographic regions and issues in the world in past and present economic, historical, and political settings.

The World in Spatial Terms

1. Identify, explain, and apply the five themes of geography (G-1A-H1)
2. Compare and contrast various types of maps (G-1A-H1)
3. Analyze or interpret a map to locate geographic information, using a variety of map elements (e.g., compass rose, symbols, distance scales, time zones, latitude, longitude) (G-1A-H1)
4. Use a city or road map to plot a route from one place to another or to identify the shortest route (G-1A-H1)
5. Construct a map based on given narrative information (e.g., location of cities, bodies of water, places of historical significance) (G-1A-H1)
6. Construct a chart, diagram, graph, or graphic organizer to display geographic information (G-1A-H1)
7. Analyze, interpret, and use information in charts, diagrams, and graphs to explain geographic issues (G-1A-H1)
8. Use maps drawn from memory to answer geographic questions (G-1A-H2)

Places and Regions

9. Identify and analyze the distinguishing physical or human characteristics of a given place (e.g., landforms, precipitation, ecosystems, settlement patterns, economic activities) (G-1B-H1)
10. Evaluate how location, topography, climate, natural resources, and other physical characteristics affect human activities (e.g., cultural diversity, migration, physical features, historical events, plantation, subsistence farming) or the significance of a place (G-1B-H1)
11. Draw conclusions about a place or area from its geographic or physical features (G-1B-H1)
12. Explain how topography, climate, soil, vegetation, and natural resources shape the history of a region (G-1B-H2)
13. Explain how location, physical features, and human characteristics of places influenced historical events (e.g., World War II, Cuban Missile Crisis, Vietnam, Middle East conflicts) (G-1B-H2)
14. Explain ways in which regional systems are interconnected (e.g., interstate transportation and trade, interconnecting rivers and canals) (G-1B-H3)
15. Analyze world regions in terms of given characteristics (e.g., population density, natural resources, economic activities, demography) (G-1B-H3)
16. Explain how physical or geographical characteristics (e.g., mountain ranges, interconnecting waterways) facilitate or hinder regional interactions (G-1B-H3)

17. Explain how technological advances have led to increasing interaction between regions (e.g., use of satellites for monitoring and exploration) (G-1B-H3)
18. Analyze how human activities and physical characteristics of regions have led to regional labels (e.g., Dust Bowl, New South, Sunbelt) (G-1B-H4)
19. Describe how physical, historical, and cultural characteristics give definition to a place or region (e.g., New South, Jerusalem) (G-1B-H4)

Physical and Human Systems

20. Categorize elements of the natural environment as belonging to one of four components of Earth's physical systems: atmosphere, lithosphere, biosphere, or hydrosphere (G-1C-H1)
21. Characterize areas or regions in terms of the physical processes that affect them (e.g., Pacific Ocean "Rim of Fire," San Andreas fault) (G-1C-H1)
22. Examine the physical effects of Earth-Sun relationships (G-1C-H1)
23. Explain the movement of wind patterns across the earth, its relationship to ocean currents, and its climatic effects on various regions of the world (G-1C-H1)
24. Examine the effects of a physical process (e.g., erosion and depository processes, global warming, El Niño) on the natural environment and societies of an area and draw conclusions from that information (G-1C-H1)
25. Compare and contrast past and present trends in human migration (G-1C-H2)
26. Assess the role of environmental changes, economic scarcity, conflict, political developments, cultural factors, and prosperity in human migration (e.g., escape from persecution or famine, migration to the suburbs) (G-1C-H2)
27. Analyze patterns of urban development in an area or region (G-1C-H3)
28. Compare, contrast, and analyze the distribution, growth rates, and other demographic characteristics of human populations in various countries or regions (G-1C-H3)
29. Analyze the current and future impact of population growth on the world (e.g., natural resources, food supply, standard of living) (G-1C-H3)
30. Analyze population pyramids and use other data, graphics, and maps to describe population characteristics of different societies and to predict future growth (G-1C-H3)
31. Compare the role that culture plays in incidents of cooperation and conflict in the present-day world (G-1C-H4)
32. Analyze how certain cultural characteristics can link or divide regions (e.g., language, religion, demography) (G-1C-H4)
33. Identify the geographical distribution of the different economic systems (market, command, traditional, mixed) (G-1C-H5)
34. Distinguish between developed and developing countries, including the standard of living in these nations, GDP, and per capita income (G-1C-H5)
35. Analyze ways in which the distribution of economic systems relates to regional tensions or regional cooperation (e.g., North and South Korea) (G-1C-H6)
36. Analyze the role of differing points of view and national self-interest in disputes over territory and resources (e.g., oil, water, boundaries) (G-1C-H6)

37. Analyze regional issues and alliances in terms of common interests related to territory and resources (e.g., oil, water, boundaries) (G-1C-H6)

Environment and Society

38. Identify technological advances that expanded human capacity to modify the environment (e.g., steam, coal, electric, nuclear power, levees) (G-1D-H1)
39. Describe challenges to human systems and activities posed by the physical environment or the impact of natural processes and disasters on human systems (e.g., infrastructure) (G-1D-H2)
40. Analyze or evaluate strategies for dealing with environmental challenges (e.g., dams or dikes to control floods, fertilizer to improve crop production) (G-1D-H2)
41. Analyze the relationship between the development of natural resources in a region and human settlement patterns or regional variations in land use (G-1D-H3)
42. Assess the ways in which unequal distribution of natural resources has led to exploration, colonization, and conflict (G-1D-H3)
43. Analyze world or regional distribution of natural resources in terms of import need and export capacity (G-1D-H3)
44. Analyze the relationship between a country's standard of living and its locally accessible natural resources (e.g., the effects of oil or natural gas reserves in a region) (G-1D-H3)
45. Describe the impact of the scarcity of natural resources (e.g., water shortage) or pollution (e.g., air, water) (G-1D-H3)
46. Assess the role of government in preserving natural resources and protecting the physical environment (G-1D-H4)
47. Evaluate the effectiveness of policies and programs related to conservation and use of natural resources (G-1D-H4)
48. Evaluate import and export policies in regard to a country's needs for resources (G-1D-H4)
49. Debate a position on an environmental issue involving conservation or use of natural resources (e.g., private vs. public interest) (G-1D-H5)
50. Evaluate options for solving a local or regional problem involving physical processes or environmental challenges (e.g., government disaster aid, environmental clean-up cost responsibility) (G-1D-H5)

Standards and Benchmarks for Teaching Civic Education and Political Science

(Recommended for Tenth Grade)

CIVICS: Citizenship and Government

FOCUS: In order for citizens to exercise their rights and fulfill their responsibilities as members of a self-governing society, they must acquire the knowledge and skills necessary for informed, responsible participation in political life. A commitment to the fundamental principles of American constitutional democracy is essential to its preservation and progression. Because a democratic society must rely on the knowledge, skills, and virtues of its citizens, the study of civics is central to the purpose of American education. The standards and benchmarks contained in this strand should be applied throughout the social studies curriculum.

STANDARD: Students develop an understanding of the structure and purposes of government, the foundations of the American democratic system, and the role of the United States in the world, while learning about the rights and responsibilities of citizenship.

BENCHMARKS 9–12: As students in grades 9–12 extend and refine their knowledge, what they know and are able to do includes:

Structure and Purposes of Government

C-1A-H1 analyzing the necessity and purposes of politics and government and identifying examples of programs that fit within those purposes; (1, 2, 4, 5)

C-1A-H2 comparing and evaluating the essential characteristics of various systems of government and identifying historical and contemporary examples of each; (1, 2, 3, 4, 5)

C-1A-H3 explaining and evaluating issues related to the distribution of powers and responsibilities within the federal system; (1, 2, 4, 5)

C-1A-H4 explaining the organization and functions of local, state, and national governments and evaluating their relationships; (1, 2, 3, 4, 5)

C-1A-H5 evaluating the role and importance of law in the American political system and applying criteria to evaluate laws; (1, 2, 3, 4, 5)

C-1A-H6 examining the major responsibilities of the national government for domestic and foreign policy; (1, 3, 4, 5)

C-1A-H7 explaining how government is financed through taxation; (1, 3, 4, 5)

Foundations of the American Political System

C-1B-H1 analyzing the central ideas and historical origins of American constitutional government and evaluating how this form of government has helped to shape American society; (1, 2, 3, 4, 5)

C-1B-H2 explaining basic democratic beliefs and principles of constitutional democracy in American society and applying them to the analysis of issues of conflicting beliefs and principles; (1, 2, 3, 4, 5)

C-1B-H3 analyzing the nature of American political and social conflict; (1, 2, 3, 4, 5)

C-1B-H4 evaluating issues related to the differences between American ideals and the realities of American social and political life; (1, 2, 4, 5)

C-1B-H5 evaluating the roles of political parties, campaigns, and elections in American politics; (1, 2, 3, 4, 5)

C-1B-H6 analyzing the historical and contemporary roles of associations and groups in local, state, and national politics; (1, 2, 3, 4, 5)

International Relationships

C-1C-H1 analyzing how the world is organized politically and evaluating how the interaction of political entities, such as nation-states and international organizations, affects the United States; (1, 2, 3, 4, 5)

C-1C-H2 analyzing the major foreign policy positions of the United States and evaluating their consequences; (1, 2, 3, 4, 5)

C-1C-H3 evaluating the impact of American ideas and actions on the world and analyzing the effects of significant international developments on the United States; (1, 2, 3, 4, 5)

Roles of the Citizen

C-1D-H1 evaluating and defending positions on issues regarding the personal, political, and economic rights of citizens; (1, 2, 3, 4, 5)

C-1D-H2 evaluating and defending positions regarding the personal and civic responsibilities of citizens in American constitutional democracy; (1, 2, 3, 4, 5)

C-1D-H3 explaining and evaluating the various forms of political participation that citizens can use to monitor and shape the formation and implementation of public policy; (1, 2, 4, 5)

C-1D-H4 analyzing and evaluating the importance of political leadership, public service, and a knowledgeable citizenry to American constitutional democracy. (1, 2, 4, 5)

Grade-Level Expectations for Teaching Civic Education and Political Science

(Recommended for Tenth Grade)

For the high school Civics course, the grade-level expectations focus on the American system of participatory government. This course serves as the culmination of the Civics instruction students have received since pre-kindergarten. It provides students with an in-depth study of the principles on which the U.S. system of government was founded, the structure of the U.S. government and how it functions, the domestic and international roles of the U.S. government, and how the U.S. government compares to other forms of government. Students are also expected to analyze and evaluate U.S. domestic and foreign policies, various laws and amendments, and the importance of participating in the American constitutional democracy.

Structure and Purposes of Government

1. Explain competing ideas about the purposes of politics and government and identify reasons why government is necessary (C-1A-H1)
2. Identify and describe services provided by government and assess their necessity and effectiveness (e.g., health care, education) (C-1A-H1)
3. Identify programs, institutions, and activities that fulfill a given governmental or political purpose (e.g., the court system, the military, revenue sharing, block grants) (C-1A-H1)
4. Analyze ways in which the purposes of the U.S. government, as defined in the U.S. Constitution, are achieved (e.g., protecting individual rights, providing for the general welfare) (C-1A-H1)
5. Compare and contrast various forms of government among nations that have been significant in U.S. history (e.g., absolute monarchy in England or France, Germany under Hitler, the Soviet Union under Stalin) (C-1A-H2)
6. Explain the distribution of powers, responsibilities, and the limits of the U.S. federal government (C-1A-H3)

7. Categorize governmental powers as delegated, reserved, concurrent, or implied (C-1A-H3)
8. Identify powers denied to federal or state governments by the U.S. Constitution (C-1A-H3)
9. Analyze or assess issues related to the distribution of powers at the federal level (e.g., tensions among the three branches of government, roles and responsibilities of the three branches) (C-1A-H3)
10. Explain the structure and functions of the three branches of the federal government, including regulatory and independent agencies and the court system (C-1A-H4)
11. Cite the roles, duties, qualifications, and terms of office for key elected and appointed officials (C-1A-H4)
12. Explain the structure and functions of state, parish, and local governments (C-1A-H4)
13. Discuss the advantages and disadvantages of various types of local government (C-1A-H4)
14. Examine constitutional provisions concerning the relationship between federal and state governments (C-1A-H4)
15. Explain the processes and strategies of how a bill becomes a law at the federal and state levels (C-1A-H5)
16. Evaluate a specific law or court ruling on given criteria (C-1A-H5)
17. Examine the meaning, implications, or applications of the U.S. Constitution (e.g., the Bill of Rights, Fourteenth Amendment) (C-1A-H5)
18. Define domestic and foreign policies (C-1A-H6)
19. Analyze responsibilities of the federal government for domestic and foreign policy (e.g. monetary policy, national defense) (C-1A-H6)
20. Analyze a past or present domestic or foreign policy issue from a news article or editorial (C-1A-H6)
21. Explain how government is financed (e.g., taxation, fines, user fees, borrowing) (C-1A-H7)
22. Identify the major sources of tax revenues at the federal, state, and local levels (C-1A-H7)
23. Analyze or evaluate various uses of tax dollars (e.g., the public's need for services versus the public's resistance to taxation) (C-1A-H7)
24. Use the rules of taxation (ability, equity, ease of payment, convenient times to pay) to analyze or evaluate a given tax practice (C-1A-H7)

Foundations of the American Political System

25. Analyze the significance of the Magna Carta, English common law, and the English Bill of Rights in creating limited government in the United States (C-1B-H1)
26. Explain how European philosophers (e.g., Rousseau, Locke, Montesquieu, Voltaire) helped shape American democratic ideas (C-1B-H1)
27. Analyze central ideas in an American historical document and explain the document's significance in shaping the U.S. Constitution (C-1B-H1)

28. Explain the meaning and importance of principles of U.S. constitutional democracy in American society (C-1B-H1)
29. Assess the importance of the U.S. Constitution as the Supreme Law of the Land, and ways in which U.S. constitutional government has helped shape American society (C-1B-H1)
30. Identify and describe examples of freedoms enjoyed today but denied to earlier Americans (C-1B-H1)
31. Explain issues involved in various compromises or plans leading to the creation of the U.S. Constitution (C-1B-H2)
32. Interpret, analyze, or apply ideas presented in a given excerpt from any political document or material (e.g., speech, essay, editorial, court case) (C-1B-H2)
33. Analyze a given example of American political or social conflict, and state and defend a position on the issue (C-1B-H3)
34. Analyze discrepancies between American ideals and social or political realities of life (e.g., equal protection vs. Jim Crow laws) (C-1B-H4)
35. Explain the two-party system and assess the role of third parties in the election process (C-1B-H5)
36. Assess the significance of campaigns, campaign finance, elections, the Electoral College, and the U.S. census in the U.S. political system (C-1B-H5)
37. Analyze the use and effects of propaganda (C-1B-H5)
38. Identify key platform positions of the major political parties (C-1B-H5)
39. Evaluate the role of the media and public opinion in American politics (C-1B-H6)
40. Explain historical and contemporary roles of special interest groups, lobbyists, and associations in U.S. politics (C-1B-H6)

International Relationships

41. Identify the political divisions of the world and the factors that contribute to those divisions (C-1C-H1)
42. Analyze and assess the various ways that nation-states interact (C-1C-H1)
43. Explain the role of the United Nations or other international organizations in political interactions and conflicts (C-1C-H1)
44. Analyze ways in which the interactions of nation-states or international organizations affect the United States (C-1C-H1)
45. Describe the means by which the United States upholds national security, protects its economic welfare and strategic interests, and attains its foreign policy objectives (e.g., aid, sanctions, embargoes, treaties) (C-1C-H2)
46. Assess the extent to which a given U.S. foreign policy position has helped or hindered the United States' relations with the rest of the world (C-1C-H2)
47. Explain how U.S. domestic policies, constitutional principles, economic behavior, and culture affect its relations with the rest of the world (C-1C-H3)
48. Describe ways in which ideas, actions, and problems of other nations impact the United States (C-1C-H3)

Roles of the Citizen

49. Distinguish between personal, political, and economic rights of citizenship (C-1D-H1)
50. Describe the importance of various rights of citizenship to the individual or to society at large (C-1D-H1)
51. Analyze an amendment or law concerning the rights of citizens in terms of their effect on public policy or American life (e.g., Nineteenth Amendment, Americans with Disabilities Act) (C-1D-H1)
52. Evaluate and defend a position on a given situation or issue in terms of the personal, political, or economic rights of citizens (C-1D-H1)
53. Assess the difference between personal and civic responsibilities (C-1D-H2)
54. Describe various forms of political participation (C-1D-H3)
55. Evaluate current and past political choices that individuals, groups, and nations have made, taking into account historical context (C-1D-H3)
56. Describe the importance of political leadership to American society, and identify ways in which citizens can exercise leadership (C-1D-H4)
57. Identify examples of public service, and describe the importance of public service to American society (C-1D-H4)
58. Evaluate the claim that American constitutional democracy requires the participation of an attentive, knowledgeable, and competent citizenry (C-1D-H4)
59. Compare and evaluate characteristics, style, and effectiveness of state and national leaders, past and present (C-1D-H4)

Standards and Benchmarks for Teaching Economics

(Recommended for Tenth Grade)

ECONOMICS: Interdependence and Decision Making

FOCUS: Effective economic education in our schools is the key to preparing young people for economic decisions in their personal lives and as citizens in a democratic society. An economically literate work force is critical to the well-being of our state and nation. Students need to understand and apply basic economic concepts in order to make reasoned judgments in a complex and changing world. With economic knowledge and decision-making skills, students will be ready to live and work productively in the 21st century. The standards and benchmarks contained in this strand should be applied throughout the social studies curriculum.

STANDARD: Students develop an understanding of fundamental economic concepts as they apply to the interdependence and decision making of individuals, households, businesses, and governments in the United States and the world.

BENCHMARKS 9–12: As students in grades 9–12 extend and refine their knowledge, what they know and are able to do includes:

Fundamental Economic Concepts

E-1A-H1 analyzing the impact of the scarcity of productive resources and examining the choices and opportunity cost that result; (1, 2, 3, 4, 5)

E-1A-H2 analyzing the roles that production, distribution, and consumption play in economic decisions; (1, 2, 3, 4)

E-1A-H3 applying the skills and knowledge necessary in making decisions about career options; (2, 3, 4, 5)

E-1A-H4 comparing and evaluating economic systems; (1, 2, 3, 4)

E-1A-H5 explaining the basic features of market structures and exchanges; (1, 3, 4)

E-1A-H6 analyzing the roles of economic institutions, such as corporations and labor unions, which compose economic systems; (1, 2, 4)

E-1A-H7 analyzing the roles of money and banking in an economic system; (1, 2, 3, 4)

E-1A-H8 applying economic concepts to understand and evaluate historical and contemporary issues; (1, 2, 3, 4)

Individuals, Households, Businesses, and Governments

E-1B-H1 identifying factors that cause changes in supply and demand; (1, 2, 3, 4)

E-1B-H2 analyzing how changes in supply and demand, price, incentives, and profit influence production and distribution in a competitive market system; (1, 2, 4)

E-1B-H3 analyzing the impact of governmental taxation, spending, and regulation on different groups in a market economy; (1, 2, 3, 4, 5)

E-1B-H4 analyzing the causes and consequences of worldwide economic interdependence; (1, 2, 3, 4)

E-1B-H5 evaluating the effects of domestic policies on international trade; (1, 2, 3, 4)

E-1B-H6 analyzing the state's role in the national and world economies; (1, 2, 3, 4, 5)

The Economy as a Whole

E-1C-H1 explaining the meanings of such economic indicators as GDP, per capita GDP, real GDP, CPI, and unemployment rate; (1, 3, 4)

E-1C-H2 explaining how interest rates, investments, and inflation/deflation impact the economy; (1, 3, 4)

E-1C-H3 analyzing the causes and consequences of unemployment, underemployment, and income distribution in a market economy; (1, 2, 3, 4)

E-1C-H4 explaining the basic concepts of United States fiscal policy, monetary policy, and regulations and describing their effects on the economy. (1, 3, 4)

Grade-Level Expectations for Teaching Economics

(Recommended for Tenth Grade)

For the high school Free Enterprise course, the grade-level expectations focus on fundamental Economics concepts, the U.S. economic system, and the international economic system from a variety of viewpoints: personal, local, national, and global. Students build on the Economics concepts learned in previous grades and learn to employ economic decision-making skills as they prepare for the world of work as producers, investors, and consumers. The role of government, international trade, and global competition are also addressed in the grade-level expectations.

1. Apply fundamental economic concepts to decisions about personal finance (E-1A-H1)

2. Define scarcity (E-1A-H1)
3. Identify factors that drive economic decisions (e.g., incentives, benefits, costs, trade-offs, consequences) (E-1A-H1)
4. Analyze an economic choice at the personal, family, or societal level to determine its opportunity cost (E-1A-H1)
5. Explain how the scarcity of natural resources leads to economic interdependence (E-1A-H1)
6. Identify the four basic economic questions (E-1A-H1)
7. Define *productivity* and characterize the relationship between productivity and standard of living (E-1A-H2)
8. Explain the role of marketing and channels of distribution in economic decisions (E-1A-H2)
9. Identify actions or conditions that increase productivity or output of the economy (E-1A-H2)
10. Explain the skills, knowledge, talents, personal characteristics, and efforts likely to enhance prospects of success in finding a job in a particular field (E-1A-H3)
11. Explain the types of jobs important to meeting the needs of Louisiana industries and an information-based society (E-1A-H3)
12. Evaluate various careers in terms of availability, educational and skill requirements, salary and benefits, and intrinsic sources of job satisfaction (E-1A-H3)
13. Compare contemporary and historic economic systems (e.g., ownership and control of production and distribution, determination of wages) (E-1A-H4)
14. Explain the advantages and disadvantages of given market structures (E-1A-H5)
15. Explain factors affecting levels of competition in a market (e.g., number of buyers and sellers, profit motive, collusion among buyers or sellers, presence of cartels) (E-1A-H5)
16. Explain the effects of competition on producers and consumers (E-1A-H5)
17. Analyze the role of various economic institutions in economic systems (E-1A-H6)
18. Explain the role of government as producer, employer, and consumer in economic systems (E-1A-H6)
19. Analyze the importance of labor-management relations and the effects of given labor and management practices on productivity or business profitability (E-1A-H6)
20. Compare and contrast characteristics of various forms of business ownership (E-1A-H6)
21. Explain ways in which businesses have changed to meet rising production costs or to compete more effectively in a global market (E-1A-H6)
22. Analyze the role of banks in economic systems (e.g., increasing the money supply by making loans) (E-1A-H7)
23. Describe the functions and purposes of the financial markets (E-1A-H7)
24. Compare and contrast credit, savings, and investment services available to the consumer from financial institutions (E-1A-H7)

25. Apply an economic concept to analyze or evaluate a given historical economic issue or situation (e.g., causes of the Great Depression, how the New Deal changed the role of the federal government) (E-1A-H8)
26. Interpret information about a current economic system undergoing change from a largely command or traditional system to a more mixed system (e.g., Eastern European countries, China, other developing economies) (E-1A-H8)
27. Explain, analyze, and apply principles of supply and demand, including concepts of price, equilibrium point, incentives, and profit (E-1B-H1)
28. Identify factors that cause changes in supply or demand for a product (e.g. complements, substitutes) (E-1B-H1)
29. Explain the role of *factors of production* in the economy (E-1B-H2)
30. Identify factors affecting production/allocation of goods/services and characterize their effects (E-1B-H2)
31. Identify the difference between monetary and non-monetary incentives and how changes in incentives cause changes in behavior (E-1B-H2)
32. Analyze the circular flow of goods and services and money payments from a diagram (E-1B-H2)
33. Identify various forms of taxation (E-1B-H3)
34. Describe the impact of given forms of taxation (E-1B-H3)
35. Describe the effects of governmental action or intervention in a market economy (E-1B-H3)
36. Describe major revenue and expenditure categories and their respective proportions of local, state, and federal budgets (E-1B-H3)
37. Predict how changes in federal spending and taxation would affect budget deficits and surpluses and the national debt (E-1B-H3)
38. Evaluate the impact of policies related to the use of resources (e.g., water use regulations, policies on scarce natural resources) (E-1B-H3)
39. Explain the causes of global economic interdependence (E-1B-H4)
40. Describe the worldwide exchange of goods and services in terms of its effect in increasing global interdependence and global competition (E-1B-H4)
41. Examine fundamental concepts of currency valuation and foreign exchange and their role in a global economy (E-1B-H4)
42. Explain how the economy of one country can affect the economies of other countries or the balance of trade among nations (E-1B-H4)
43. Explain the role of the International Monetary Fund in supporting world economies (E-1B-H4)
44. Identify and evaluate various types of trade barriers among nations (E-1B-H5)
45. Take and defend a position on a trade policy or issue (e.g., NAFTA, G8, European Union) (E-1B-H5)
46. Evaluate the role and importance of Louisiana ports and products in the national and international economy (E-1B-H6)
47. Explain the meaning or use of various economic indicators and their implications as measures of economic well-being (E-1C-H1)

48. Define productivity and characterize the relationship between productivity and standard of living (E-1C-H1)
49. Interpret various economic indicators used in a chart, table, or news article (E-1C-H1)
50. Draw conclusions about two different economies based on given economic indicators (E-1C-H1)
51. Explain how inflation and deflation are reflected in the Consumer Price Index (E-1C-H2)
52. Explain the impact of inflation/deflation on individuals, nations, and the world, including its impact on economic decisions (E-1C-H2)
53. Describe the effects of interest rates on businesses and consumers (E-1C-H2)
54. Predict the consequences of investment decisions made by individuals, businesses, and government (E-1C-H2)
55. Predict how interest rates will act as an incentive for savers and borrowers (E-1C-H2)
56. Explain various causes and consequences of unemployment in a market economy (E-1C-H3)
57. Analyze regional, national, or demographic differences in rates of unemployment (E-1C-H3)
58. Analyze the relationship between the business cycle and employment (E-1C-H3)
59. Explain the meaning of *underemployment* and analyze its causes and consequences (E-1C-H3)
60. Explain factors contributing to unequal distribution of income in a market economy (E-1C-H3)
61. Interpret a chart or graph displaying various income distributions (e.g., in the United States vs. the Third World, various groups within a country) (E-1C-H3)
62. Distinguish monetary policy from fiscal policy (E-1C-H4)
63. Explain the role of the Federal Reserve System as the central banking system of the United States (E-1C-H4)
64. Explain the role of regulatory agencies in the U.S. economy (E-1C-H4)
65. Explain the role of the Federal Deposit Insurance Corporation (FDIC) (E-1C-H4)

Note

[1] Adapted from the Louisiana State Department of Education (http://www.doe.state.la.us/lde/ssa/2108.html).

Section VI

Basic Instructional Considerations

When planning for instructional delivery, there are several topics worthy of consideration. Among those, we will consider management and discipline techniques (including eleven techniques for better classroom discipline), Edgar Dale's Cone of Experience, using discussion in teaching, teaching critical thinking skills, the wisdom of having high expectations of our students, how to teach important reading skills in social studies content material, teaching current events, and assessment (including rubrics, testing, and developing performance assessments).

Management and Discipline [1]

Thomas McDaniel (1986) suggests eleven techniques for better classroom discipline:

1. *Focusing*. Be sure you have the attention of everyone in your classroom before you start your lesson. Don't attempt to teach over the chatter of students who are not paying attention. Inexperienced teachers sometimes think that by beginning their lesson, the class will settle down. The students will see that things are underway now and it is time to go to work. Sometimes this works, but the students are also going to think that you are willing to compete with them. You don't mind talking while they talk. You are willing to speak louder so that they can finish their conversation even after you have started the lesson. They get the idea that you accept their inattention and that it is permissible to talk while you are presenting a lesson.

The focusing technique means that you will demand their attention before you begin. That you will wait and not start until everyone has settled down. Experienced teachers know that silence on their part is very effective. They will punctuate their waiting by extending it 5 to 10 seconds after the classroom is completely quiet. Then they begin their lesson using a quieter voice than normal. A soft spoken teacher often has a calmer, quieter classroom than one with a stronger voice. The students sit still in order to hear what the teacher says.

2. *Direct instruction*. Uncertainty increases the level of negative (unproductive) excitement in the classroom. The technique of direct instruction is to begin each class by telling the students exactly what will be happening. The teacher outlines what the students and teacher will be doing this period. The teacher may set time limits for some tasks.

An effective way to marry this technique with the first one is to include time at the end of the period for students to do activities of their choosing. The teacher may finish the description of the hour's activities with: "And I think we will have some time at the end of the period for you to chat with your friends, go to the library, or catch up on work for other classes."

The teacher is more willing to wait for class attention when she or he knows there is extra time to meet the day's goals and objectives. The students soon realize that the more time the teacher waits for their attention, the less free time they have at the end of the hour.

3. *Monitoring*. The key to this principle is to circulate. Get up and get around the room. While your students are working, make the rounds. Check on their progress.

An effective teacher will make a pass through the whole room about two minutes after the students have started a written assignment. The teacher checks to see that each student has started, that the students are on the correct page, and that everyone has put their names on their papers. The delay is important. The teacher wants the students to have a problem or two finished so she or he can check that answers are correctly labeled or in complete sentences. The effective teacher then circulates, checks for understanding, and provides individualized instruction and assistance as needed. Students who are not yet quite on task will be quick to get going as they see the teacher approach. Those that were distracted or slow to get started can be nudged along.

The teacher does not interrupt the class or try to make general announcements about the task unless she or he notices that several students have difficulty with the same thing. The teacher uses a quiet voice and the students appreciate the personal and positive attention.

4. *Modeling*. It is often said that "values are caught and not taught." Teachers who are courteous, prompt, enthusiastic, in control, patient, and

An effective teacher circulates through the whole room, checks for understanding, and provides for individualized instruction as needed.

organized provide examples for their students through their own behavior. The "do as I say, not as I do" teachers send mixed messages that confuse students and invite misbehavior.

If you want students to use quiet voices in your classroom while they work, you too will use a quiet voice as you move through the room helping youngsters.

5. *Nonverbal cuing*. A standard item in the classroom of the fifties was the clerk's bell. A shiny nickel bell sat on the teacher's desk. With one tap of the button on top, the teacher had everyone's attention. Teachers have shown a lot of ingenuity over the years in making use of nonverbal cues in the classroom. Some flip light switches. Others keep clickers in their pockets.

Nonverbal cues can also be facial expressions, body posture, and hand signals. Care should be given in choosing the types of cues you use in your classroom. Take time to explain what you want the student to do when you use your cues. Harry Wong's book, *The First Days of School* (2004), is the preeminent book on classroom management and provides the new teacher with excellent strategies for establishing routines and procedures for managing the classroom. It contains good ideas for nonverbal cuing.

6. *Environmental control*. A classroom can be a warm, cheery place. Students enjoy an environment that changes periodically. Study centers with pictures and color invite enthusiasm for your subject.

Young people like to know about you and your interests. Include personal items in your classroom. A family picture or a few items from a hobby or collection on your desk will trigger personal conversations with your students. As they get to know you better, you will see fewer problems with discipline.

Just as you may want to enrich your classroom, there are times when you may want to impoverish it as well. You may need a quiet corner with few distractions. Some students will get caught up in visual exploration. For them, the splash and the color are a "siren song" that pulls them off task. They may need more vanilla and less rocky-road. Have a place where you can steer such a youngster. Let him get his work done first and then come back to explore and enjoy the rest of the room.

7. *Low-profile intervention*. Most students are sent to the principal's office as a result of confrontational escalation. The teacher has called them on a lesser offense, but in the moments that follow, the student and the teacher are swept up in a verbal maelstrom. Much of this can be avoided when the teacher's intervention is quiet and calm.

An effective teacher will take care that the student is not rewarded for misbehavior by becoming the focus of attention. The effective teacher monitors the activity in the classroom, moving around the room. The teacher anticipates problems before they occur. The teacher's approach to a misbehaving student is inconspicuous. Others in the class are not distracted.

While lecturing to the class, a wise teacher makes effective use of name dropping. If the teacher sees a student talking or off task, she or he simply drops the youngster's name into the dialog in a natural way: "And you see, David, Alexander's horse played a significant role in his battlefield successes." David hears his name and is drawn back on task. The rest of the class doesn't seem to notice.

8. *Assertive discipline.* This is traditional limit-setting authoritarianism. When executed as presented by Lee Canter (1992) (who has made this form of discipline one of the most widely known and practiced), it will include a good mix of praise. This is high-profile discipline. The teacher is the boss and no student has the right to interfere with the learning of any other student. Clear rules are laid out and consistently enforced.

9. *Assertive I-messages.* A component of assertive discipline, these I-messages are statements that the teacher uses when confronting a student who is misbehaving. They are intended to be clear descriptions of what the student is supposed to do. The inexperienced teacher may incorrectly try: "I want you to stop . . ." only to discover that this usually triggers confrontation and denial. The focus is on the misbehavior and the student is quick to retort: "I wasn't doing anything!" or "It wasn't my fault . . ." or "Since when is there a rule against . . ." and escalation has begun. The teacher who makes good use of this technique will focus the child's attention first and foremost on the behavior he wants, not on the misbehavior: "I want you to . . ." or "I need you to . . ." or "I expect you to . . . ."

10. *Humanistic I-messages.* These I-messages are expressions of our feelings. Thomas Gordon (2003), creator of *Teacher Effectiveness Training* (TET), tells us to structure these messages in three parts. First, a description of the student's behavior, "When you talk while I talk . . ."; second, the effect this behavior has on the teacher, ". . . I have to stop my teaching . . ."; and third, the feeling that it generates in the teacher, ". . . which frustrates me."

A teacher, distracted by a student who was constantly talking while he tried to teach, once made this powerful expression of feelings: "I can not imagine what I have done to you that I do not deserve the respect from you that I get from the others in this class. If I have been rude to you or inconsiderate in any way, please let me know. I feel as though I have somehow offended you and now you are unwilling to show me respect." The student did not talk during his lectures again for many weeks.

11. *Positive discipline.* Use classroom rules that describe the behaviors you want instead of listing things the students cannot do. Instead of "no running in the room," use "move through the building in an orderly manner." Instead of "no fighting," use "settle conflicts appropriately." Instead of "no gum chewing," use "leave gum at home." Refer to your rules as expectations. Let your students know this is how you expect them to behave in your classroom. Make ample use of praise. When you see good behavior, acknowledge it. This can be done verbally, of course, but it doesn't have to be. A nod, a smile or a "thumbs up" will reinforce the behavior.

Dale's Cone of Experience

Dale's Cone of Experience (figure 6.1) is helpful in planning experiences which range from the concrete to the more abstract. Concrete experiences include hands-on, student-participatory activities, while abstract experiences include oral lectures.

Figure 6.1 Dale's Cone of Experience

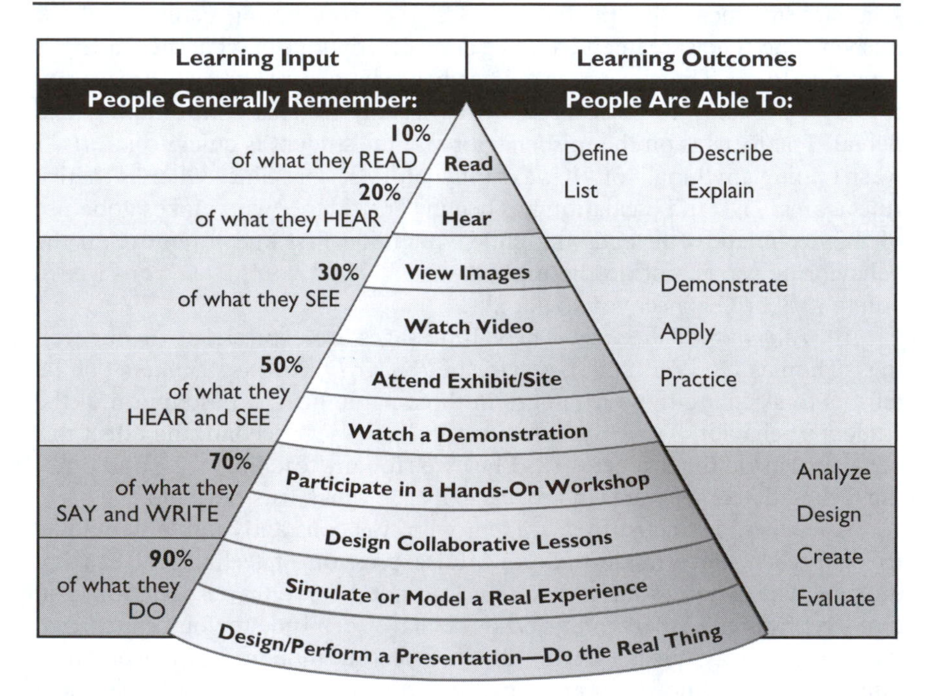

Source: Adapted from Edgar Dale (1969), *Audiovisual methods in teaching*. Belmont, CA: International Thomson Publishing.

Using Discussion in Teaching

Teachers open the door. You enter by yourself.

—Chinese Proverb

Teaching by discussion[2] can be an extremely effective means of helping students apply abstract ideas and think critically about what they are learning. In his now classic study, Benjamin Bloom (1953) concluded that when the purpose of a class is to develop problem-solving skills and abilities, the least efficient discussion is superior to most lectures. However, fostering effective discussion is difficult—even for experienced teachers—and especially with larger classes.

Teachers who frequently practice both discussion and lecture report that leading an effective discussion takes greater preparation than does preparing a lecture. Like a lecture, an effective discussion has a beginning, a middle, and an end that are all determined by the agenda for a particular session. Unlike the lecture, however, this process is not controlled by one individual's presentation. Rather, the discussion leader must walk a fine line between controlling the group and letting its members speak. The most common pitfalls in a discussion—all exacerbated by lack of organization and clearly defined goals—are overly long digressions, pointless arguments, or no real discussion at all. The advantages of discussion teaching include helping students develop higher-order reasoning skills such as analysis, synthesis, and evaluation, as well as developing motivation and enthusiasm for a subject. In providing an opportunity for the members of the class to work actively with the ideas and the concepts that are being pursued, discussion teaching has the added benefit of providing immediate feedback to the teacher about student learning.

Discussion requires that students place their opinions, conclusions, and questions before the rest of the class. This prospect can be intimidating, especially for less mature students. Therefore, in order for good discussion to take place, you need to create a comfortable and nonthreatening environment.

Get acquainted. Just as it is important that you know who your students are, it is also important for students to know each other so that they feel comfortable talking in front of their peers. This can be done early in the school year by having students give short 2–3 minute talks about themselves—their likes, dislikes, hobbies, favorite music, favorite entertainment, and so on.

Show respect for all questions and comments. It is the important to avoid judging student responses so that students are never embarrassed by asking or answering a question. As one experienced teacher said, "You have to provide a safe and welcome atmosphere for students to make mistakes, to make fools of themselves, to be wrong, and to disagree." You should avoid making evaluative comments or simply negating a student's response by turning to another student with exactly the same question. If your responses to student comments and questions reinforce their validity, students will be more willing to take the risk required to participate.

Integrate student responses into the discussion. Students will commonly participate more freely in discussions when they feel their own concerns and ideas have contributed to the agenda. Instead of evaluative comments like "That's good," try to restate the critical portions of the comments and to connect them with the main points under discussion. After the first student presents an opinion, pose follow-up questions, such as, "How do the rest of you feel about it?" You must make it clear that the students should listen to each other and not just to you.

What Kinds of Questions Will Promote Discussion?

In large part, you control the progress of a discussion by controlling the kinds of questions you pose. Remember, a discussion is not just to test that they've read the book. Simply asking for information retrieval will kill a discussion. If the goal is to get them to think critically and creatively, you need to ask questions that demand that kind of response.

Start with an open-ended question. You can get a discussion going and people talking by asking open-ended questions such as, "What did you think about Alexander the Great's boyhood?" Or, "What struck you as most problematic about the Ptolemy's view of the world?" "What things would you have enjoyed most about life in ancient Greece? Least?" These types of questions have several advantages. First, because they invite students' opinions, they decrease the odds that your question will be met with an awkward silence. Second, because they encourage multiple viewpoints, they also lessen the problem of having the brightest—or most vocal—student dominate the class. Finally, by asking students to pinpoint problems and crucial issues, they provide the beginnings of further topics for discussion.

Ask questions with multiple answers. Perhaps the most straightforward method of encouraging participation from as many people as possible is to ask questions with multiple rather than single answers. Divergent yet focused questions remove students' fear of not getting the "right" answer. For example, instead of asking, "Why is the ending of *Wuthering Heights* a good one?" you could ask, "What are other ways in which Emily Brontë might have ended *Wuthering Heights*?" Although these questions may not seem useful because they don't call for factual information, they are extremely valuable because they force students to examine and integrate the information they have and to reach some kind of conclusion that the facts will support. In other words, they promote critical thinking.

Make sure that everyone has a chance to contribute. Once you pose a question, you must pause long enough for someone to pick it up—and not necessarily the first person who raises a hand. Reward for rapid answering promotes the programmed answer even to an opinion question. You might occasionally try having students write down an answer first, which gives more reticent students a chance to articulate their thoughts before speaking.

Discussion can be a centerpiece of history and social studies teaching. Observers of history classrooms have long remarked that discussions serve as the staple of history and social studies instruction.

Four Variations of Discussion

- *Recitation.* Students regurgitate textbook information in response to teachers' predictable questions.
- *Blather.* Students express opinions without feeling compelled to explain the reasons for their beliefs. Opinions are plentiful; evidence is sparse. The blather consists of one student saying, "I believe. . . ." followed by a series of other students' belief statements. Students do not listen to each other; nor do they feel listening is necessary.
- *Debate.* Students defend a position, which is sometimes assigned. It begins with the teacher asking an evaluative question: Should the

United States withdraw from post-occupation Iraq? Should the South have seceded from the Union? Should the Cartheginian, Hannibal, have crossed the Alps and invaded the Roman Empire? Such questions are provocative and invite students to take positions and to support those positions. A poorly prepared teacher will rely on a textbook and quickly discover that most textbooks provide only a thin narrative description. Unless students are well prepared, this technique can lead to mere arguing or ill-informed, rambling discussions.

- *Deliberative discussion.* Involves students in reasoning and choice and requires you and your students to engage in a rigorous discourse in which sources, ideas, values, and conversations are held up to analysis. Deliberation cultivates reasoning and choice while also fostering virtues necessary in a democratic society. Deliberative discussion fosters a habit of mind that suspends judgments before making rash decisions. It encourages students to suspend their evaluations of historical documents, artifacts, or incidents until they have had a chance to thoroughly examine the meaning of these sources.

Teaching Critical Thinking[3]

> It is possible to store the mind with a million facts and still be entirely uneducated.
>
> —Alec Bourne

Critical thinking skills figure prominently among the goals for education, whether one asks developers of curricula, educational researchers, parents, or employers. Although there are some quite diverse definitions of critical thinking, nearly all emphasize the ability and tendency to gather, evaluate, and use information effectively. Across all subject areas and levels, there are several discrete skills related to an overall ability for critical thinking, which include:

- Finding analogies and other kinds of relationships between pieces of information,
- Determining the relevance and validity of information that could be used for structuring and solving problems, and
- Finding and evaluating solutions or alternative ways of treating problems.

Just as there are similarities among the definitions of critical thinking across subject areas and levels, there are several generally recognized "hallmarks" of teaching for critical thinking, which include:

- *Promoting interaction among students as they learn.* Learning in a group setting often helps each member achieve more.
- *Asking open-ended questions that do not assume the "one right answer."* Critical thinking is often exemplified best when the problems are inherently ill-defined and do not have a "right" answer. Open-ended questions

also encourage students to think and respond creatively, without fear of giving the "wrong" answer.

- *Allowing sufficient time for students to reflect on the questions asked or problems posed.* Critical thinking seldom involves snap judgments; therefore, posing questions and allowing adequate time before soliciting responses helps students understand that they are expected to deliberate and to ponder, and that the immediate response is not always the best response.
- *Teaching for transfer.* The skills for critical thinking should "travel well." They generally will do so only if teachers provide opportunities for students to see how a newly acquired skill can apply to other situations and to the students' own experience.

Building Categories

Students often are given (and asked to memorize) explicit rules for classifying information. For example, there is a set of criteria for determining whether a word is being used as a noun or as a verb. The *building categories strategy*, however, is an inductive reasoning tool that helps students categorize information by discovering the rules rather than merely memorizing them. Such active learning typically results in better understanding and better retention of the concepts and related material than is possible with a more directive teaching method.

For example, students can distinguish between *discoveries* and *inventions*. Students work in two groups (Discoveries Group and Inventions Group). Worksheets prepared in advance ask for information about who, what, when, where, how, etc., of several different discoveries and inventions. Once the information is collected, it is compiled into large wall charts (one for Discoveries, one for Inventions).

At this point, some questions can be posed to both groups at once: What are the similarities among the members of each group? What are the differences between the two groups? How could the following statement be completed: "A discovery is different from an invention because. . . ." The teacher provides appropriate feedback throughout, using open-ended questions to help students identify inadequate or inaccurate categorization rules. Finally, the students are allowed to test the "generalizability" of their proposed rules by looking at new instances and placing them in the appropriate category.

The strategy is described here in the context of a social studies problem, but it can work equally well in other disciplines and with more abstract categories. For example, students in science can learn the rules for "arachnids" versus "crustaceans," and students of jurisprudence can discover the differences between "felonies" and "misdemeanors."

Finding Problems

One of the most important practical thinking skills one can acquire is knowing how to identify a problem. The *finding problems strategy* is a way of framing tasks so that students use skills similar to those needed for the ill-defined problems they will encounter in life. A sugar cane farmer in Louisiana wants to know the best way for him to get his sugar to market. River barges? Railroads? Eighteen-wheelers? Students work in collaborative groups to investigate such things as cost, volume, and speed. This is a problem for which the available data will render a plausible solution. What about other problems that are less solvable but offer intriguing and inviting student research efforts? Some examples would be the world AIDS crisis, the depletion of the rain forests, the extraction of energy resources and the resultant damage to the Earth, the continuing development of giant cities in the world and their corresponding infrastructure problems.

Problem finding is an excellent group activity, particularly if two or more groups work on the same task independently and then come together to compare strategies. In this way, each student has the benefit of exposure to several ways of solving the problem.

Enhancing the Environment

Critical thinking in the classroom is facilitated by a physical and intellectual environment that encourages a spirit of discovery. The physical layout of the classroom can enhance critical thinking. If seating is arranged so that students share the "stage" with the teacher and all can see and interact with each other, this helps to minimize the passive, receptive mode many students adopt when all are facing the teacher. Visual aids in the classroom can encourage ongoing attention to critical thought processes (e.g., posting signs that say, "Why do I think that?" "Is it fact or opinion?" "How are these two things alike?" "What would happen if . . .?"). Suggestions below each of the questions can remind students how they should go about answering them. Most importantly, as the students move through the curriculum in a given subject, their attention can be directed periodically to the signs as appropriate. In this way, the signs emphasize the idea of transfer by showing that many of the same thinking strategies and skills apply to different topics and problems.

Having High Expectations[4]

Nearly all schools claim to hold high expectations for all students. In reality, however, what is professed is not always practiced. Although some schools and teachers maintain uniformly high expectations for all students, others have "great expectations" for particular segments of the student population but minimal expectations for others. In many urban and inner city schools, low expectations predominate.

Some say that our current ceiling for students is really much closer to where the floor ought to be. There is, to many, a great disparity between what students are learning and what they are capable of learning.

A good deal of evidence suggests that schools can improve student learning by encouraging teachers and students to set their sights high, to expect more. "You get what you expect," say some. "If you expect a lot, you get a lot. If you don't expect much, you don't get much."

The expectations teachers have for their students and the assumptions they make about their potential have a tangible effect on student achievement. Teacher expectations seem to play a significant role in determining how well and how much students learn. Students tend to internalize the beliefs teachers have about their ability. Generally, they go up to the level or down to the level their teachers expect of them. If teachers show that they believe in students, students tend to believe in themselves.

Conversely, when students are viewed as lacking in ability or motivation and are not expected to make significant progress, they tend to adopt this perception of themselves. Regrettably, some students, particularly those from certain social, economic, or ethnic groups, discover that their teachers consider them lacking in ability. They find that their teachers don't think they can handle demanding learning tasks, so that's how they begin to perceive themselves.

Teachers' expectations for students—whether high or low—can become a self-fulfilling prophecy. That is, students tend to give to teachers as much or as little as teachers expect of them. A characteristic shared by most highly effective teachers is their adherence to uniformly high expectations. They don't alter their attitudes or expectations for their students, regardless of a student's race or ethnicity, life experiences, interests, or socioeconomic status.

Either consciously or unconsciously, teachers often behave differently toward students based on the beliefs and assumptions they have about them. For example, studies have found that teachers engage in affirming nonverbal behaviors such as smiling, leaning toward, and making eye contact with students more frequently when they believe they are dealing with high-ability students than when they believe they are interacting with less capable students.

Students who are perceived to be low in ability may also be given fewer opportunities to learn new material, asked less stimulating questions, given briefer and less informative feedback, praised less frequently for success, called on less frequently, and given less time to respond than students who are considered high in ability. In addition, instructional content is sometimes "dumbed down" for students considered to be low in ability. Students in low groups or who are thought of by the teacher as less capable are usually offered less exciting and stimulating instruction, less emphasis on meaning and conceptualization, and more rote drill and practice activities than those students for whom the teacher has higher expectations. When teachers summarily categorize or label students, it is often the case that some students end up receiving a watered-down curriculum along with less intense, less motivating instruction.

In today's schools, many subscribe to a philosophy of *educational predestination*. Poor performance in school is often attributed to low ability, and ability is viewed as being immune to alteration, much like eye or skin color. Therefore, poorly performing students often come to believe that no matter how much effort they put forth, it will not be reflected in improved performance.

This view contrasts sharply with the predominant perspective in many other cultures, where hard work and effort are considered key to students' academic achievement. In these cultures, high expectations are maintained for all students, and if a student is not succeeding, it is attributed to lack of effort and hard work, not to insufficient intellectual ability.

Tracking and ability grouping can also affect expectations. A criticism of traditional tracking is that expectations for students as well as pace of instruction are reduced in lower ability groups. A large number of studies from a wide range of years suggest that ability grouping appears to be detrimental for low-ability students and impedes the progress of students in lower groups. Mixed-age and mixed-ability classes, in contrast, have been shown to improve achievement, perhaps in part because more is expected from students in such groups.

Although students may appear to accept or even relish lax teachers with low standards, they ultimately come away with more respect for teachers who believe in them enough to demand more, both academically and behaviorally. In a national survey of over 1,300 high school students, students were asked on questionnaires and in focus group discussions what they think of and want from their schools. Students' responses concerning what they want were clustered in three main areas:

- *A yearning for order.* They complained about lax instructors and unenforced rules. Many felt insulted at the minimal demands placed upon them. They stated unequivocally that they would work harder if more were expected of them.
- *A yearning for structure.* They expressed a desire for closer monitoring and watchfulness from teachers. In addition, very significant numbers of students wanted after-school classes for those who were failing.
- *A yearning for moral authority.* Although students acknowledged that cheating was commonplace, they indicated that they wanted schools to teach ethical values such as honesty and hard work.

Because there are so many indications that teachers' expectations have a direct bearing on their students, a sort of "self-fulfilling prophecy," teachers should routinely project positive attitudes and high expectations for all students. They should behave toward all students in ways that indicate to the students that they view them as eager learners with the same sort of enthusiasm for learning as the teacher has. To the extent that a teacher expects a lot, the teacher is more likely to get a lot. When teachers and administrators maintain high expectations, they encourage in students a desire to aim high rather than to slide by. To expect less is to do students a disservice, not a favor.

Teaching Reading Skills

Reading is the chief avenue to information needed in learning social studies. Reading is the major way that students search for information in content material. Every teacher needs to be knowledgeable about reading skills and how to teach them, along with the teaching of content material. Reading instruction must go hand-in-hand with the teaching of content material in an interdisciplinary social studies program. The best technique, the most productive strategy for teaching reading skills in content material, is to teach skills as the need arises. The best time to teach a student a reading skill is when he or she needs it, and that frequently occurs in content reading material.

Perhaps the simplest definition of reading is: getting the idea from the author's head to the reader's head. To do this successfully, there are two crucial functions involved: word perception and comprehension. Figure 6.2 shows the components of these two essentials in the reading process.

Word perception involves the process of decoding, deciphering, or unlocking unknown words. Sometimes called word recognition or word identification, it is a twofold process that includes both the identification of printed symbols and the attachment of meaning to the printed symbols. Without word perception, there is no reading. It is the foundation of the reading process.

Students need word perception skills that allow them to explore a variety of resource materials in social studies classes, including textbooks, trade books, journals, magazines, pamphlets, reference books, and specialized publications, as well as charts, graphs, and other materials. The best way to teach these vital skills is in material that represents real reading instead of isolated drill. Word perception skills should be taught in material that is highly motivational to the student.

Figure 6.2 Components of the Reading Process

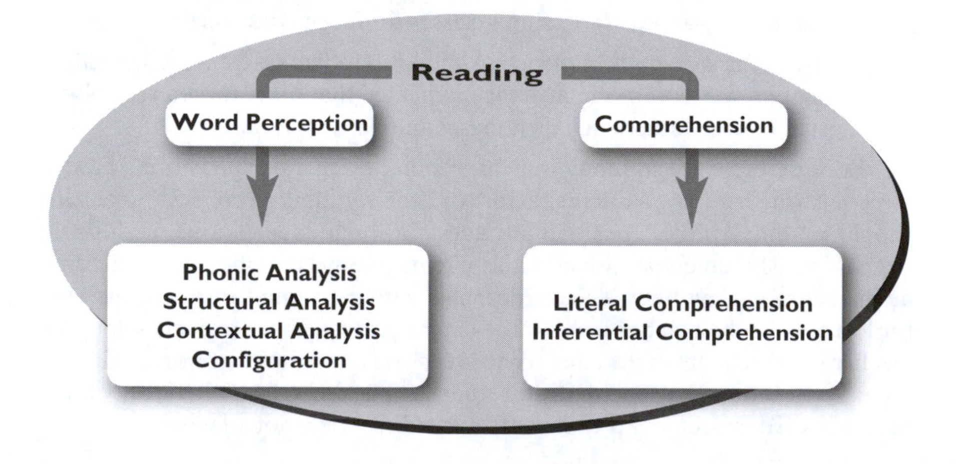

Students who become effective readers must be able to use word perception techniques whenever they need to unlock an unknown word. Like touch typing, the skills of word perception go to work for the reader, automatically and in concert with one another, whenever they are needed to decode an unknown word. This is called the *theory of automaticity.*

While word perception is vital in the reading process, it is *comprehension* that allows us to get the idea from the author's head to the reader's head. The main purpose of reading is comprehending and understanding what the author had in mind; to grasp and understand the meaning of what has been written. Comprehension requires thinking.

Comprehension skills are developed throughout life. As teachers work with students to improve comprehension skills, it is important to present a balance between literal comprehension and inferential comprehension. Opportunities for students to engage in the higher-order thinking required in interpreting, reading critically, and reading creatively are important for inclusion in the content-area reading program.

SQ3R Technique

One of the most effective aids to comprehension ever devised is the SQ3R procedure. It was not known as a metacognitive procedure (*metacognition* means knowledge of cognition or knowledge of thought processes) when it was originally described by Frances Robinson. Since that time a number of variations have been devised. However, none of these has proven more successful than Robinson's original technique.

SQ3R stands for *survey, question, read, recite,* and *review.* This method is best adapted to material in which subject headings are used, as in social studies and science books.

- *Survey.* The student reads the introductory sentences at the beginning of the chapter and then all boldface headings, captions, and questions at the end of the chapter. Students who use this technique should at first be timed to make sure they only survey. They have a tendency to read the material as they have been doing if they are not put under some time pressure. Two to three minutes is usually sufficient; however, time will depend on the age and proficiency of the readers and the length of the chapter.
- *Question.* Each heading is turned into a question. For example, in a social studies book a heading says: Vasco da Gama Sails to India. In this stage of SQ3R, this changes to, When did Vasco da Gama sail to India? or Why did Vasco da Gama sail to India? When students first use this technique, you should help them devise questions. One way is to develop a list of common beginnings for questions such as, When did, Why are, Why did, and Why is.
- *Read.* Students read down to the next boldface heading to find the answer to the question.

- *Recite.* After reading, the student looks up from the book and attempts to answer the question. When students are first learning this technique, this can be done orally as a class procedure. After they have had a chance to practice, they should recite silently to themselves. If a student cannot answer a question, he or she should read the material under that boldface heading again.
- *Review.* After the entire chapter has been read, students go back and read only the questions derived from the boldface headings and see if they can answer them. If any questions cannot be answered, they would read the material under that question again.

Teaching Current Events

The media are all powerful. They shape our ideas about every person, place, and thing with whom or with which we are not personally acquainted. Following are five techniques and resources for effective teaching about the media.

1. *Daily discussion of news.* This helps students relate "school learning" to life outside of school. Meaningful bridges can be built between life in and out of school and between the past and present.
2. *News clippings from the newspaper and news magazines.* Students should regularly clip interesting items from newspapers and news magazines and make reports to the class. Often, students can create PowerPoint presentations for making their reports. Too, they can frequently work in pairs or small groups to create their news media reports.
3. *News map–bulletin board.* This learning tool is truly needed in every class. Place a large world map adjacent to some bulletin board space. When students bring in articles they have clipped from newspapers and news magazines, the article can be placed on the bulletin board with a piece of yarn connecting the article to the place on the world map where the event took place. This is a good way for students to maintain a continuing global perspective.
4. *Classroom newspapers (pros and cons).* Although classroom newspapers allow everyone in class to see the same articles and the same graphics, they are expensive and are not as current as newspapers and news magazines. With today's access to the Internet, newspapers, cartoons, and graphics from all over the world can be easily accessed.
5. *Newspaper in Education (NIE).* This program, sponsored by newspaper publishers, is for teachers and is usually conducted in the summer months, when school is not in session. Generally, the program takes the form of a one-day workshop in which teachers are given expert help in techniques and strategies for using the daily newspaper as an instructional tool. NIE workshops are excellent opportunities for

teachers to learn up-to-date ideas for teaching current events in the social studies classroom. Visit the NIE Web site for more information (http://nieonline.com/).

Students can use the following checklist when preparing news reports from clippings:

- Note the main ideas.
- Select the most important facts.
- Have pictures or other items to show.
- Be ready to locate the event on a map.
- Be ready to answer questions.
- If possible, relate it to a topic under study.

Good journalists know that every well-written news story needs five components (*who*, *what*, *where*, *when*, and *why/how*). Students can examine news reports to find the five essential components of a news article. By dissecting news articles, students will be able to more accurately ascertain whether the article contains unwanted information, such as opinions, and how to differentiate between fact and opinion. In addition, the dissecting procedure will allow students to identify background information appearing in the article. Use a five-column chart with "the five Ws" as headings to teach your students to dissect news articles in order to find the five essential components.

Comparing Newspapers and Television News

This activity, which has students compare the news coverage in newspapers and network television, may be used over several days and take the form of a group task (see table 6.1). It may lead you to ideas for similar activities for your particular students.

Table 6.1 Network News versus Newspaper Activity (in percentage)

Subject	Network Morning News	Network Evening News	Newspaper
Government			
Foreign Affairs			
Defense/Military			
Domestic Affairs			
Crime			
Business			
Celebrities/Entertainment			
Lifestyle			
Science			
Accidents/Disasters			
Other			

Five Major Trends in the Media Landscape[5]

1. *There are now several models of journalism, and the trajectory increasingly is toward those that are faster, looser, and cheaper.* The traditional press model—the journalism of verification—is one in which journalists are concerned first with trying to substantiate facts. It has ceded ground for years on talk shows and cable to a new journalism of assertion, where information is offered with little time and little attempt to independently verify its veracity. Consider the allegations by the "Swift Boat Veterans for Truth," and the weeks of reporting required to find that their claims were unsubstantiated. The blogosphere, while adding the richness of citizen voices, expands this culture of assertion exponentially, and brings to it an affirmative philosophy: publish anything, especially points of view, and the reporting and verification will occur afterward in the response of fellow bloggers. The result is sometimes true and sometimes false. Blogs helped unmask errors at CBS, but also spread the unfounded conspiracy theory that the GOP stole the presidential election in Ohio. All this makes it easier for those who would manipulate public opinion—government, interest groups and corporations—to deliver unchecked messages, through independent outlets or their own faux-news Web sites, video and text news releases and paid commentators. Next, computerized editing has the potential to take this further, blending all these elements into a mix.
2. *The rise in partisanship of news consumption and the notion that people have retreated to their ideological corners for news has been widely exaggerated.* In the journalism of affirmation, the news is gathered with a point of view, whether acknowledged or not, and audiences come to have their preconceptions reinforced. In 2004, that notion gained new force when Pew Research Center survey data revealed that Republicans and conservatives had become more distrustful of the news media over the past four years, while the perceptions of Democrats, moderates, and liberals had remained about the same. This led to the popular impression that independent journalism was giving way to a European-style partisan press, in which some Americans consume Red Media and others Blue. The evidence suggests that such perceptions are greatly overstated. The overwhelming majority of Americans say they prefer independent, nonpartisan news media. So, apparently, do advertisers and investors. In addition, distrusting the media does not correlate to how or whether people use it. Not only do Republicans and Democrats consume most news media outlets in similar levels, but those in both parties who distrust the news media are often heavier consumers of news outlets than those who are more trusting. The only exceptions to this are talk radio and cable news. In the latter, Republicans have tended to congregate in one place, Fox. For most other media, the political orientation of the audience mirrors the population. The polit-

ical makeup of the network news audience, for instance, matches that of the Weather Channel.

3. *To adapt, journalism may have to move in the direction of making its work more transparent and more expert, and of widening the scope of its searchlight.* Journalists aspire in the new landscape to be the one source that can best help citizens discover what to believe and what to disbelieve—a shift from the role of gatekeeper to that of authenticator or referee. To do that, however, it appears news organizations may have to make some significant changes. They may have to document their reporting process more openly so that audiences can decide for themselves whether to trust it. Doing so would help inoculate their work from the rapid citizen review that increasingly will occur online and elsewhere. In effect, the era of trust-me journalism has passed, and the era of show-me journalism has begun. As they move toward being authenticators, news organizations also may have to enrich their expertise, both on staff and in their reporting. Since citizens have a deeper range of information at their fingertips, the level of proof in the press must rise accordingly. The notion of filling newsrooms only with talented generalists may not be enough. And rather than merely monitoring the official corridors of power, news organizations may need to monitor the new alternative means of public discussion as well. How else can the press referee what people are hearing in those venues? Such changes will require experimentation, investment, vision and a reorganization of newsrooms.
4. *Despite the new demands, there is more evidence than ever that the mainstream media are investing only cautiously in building new audiences.* That is true even online, where audiences are growing. The data suggest that news organizations have imposed more cutbacks in their Internet operations than in their old media, and where the investment has come is in technology for processing information, not people to gather it. One reason is that the new technologies are still providing relatively modest revenues. The problem is that the traditional media are leaving it to technology companies—like Google—and to individuals and entrepreneurs—like bloggers—to explore and innovate on the Internet. The risk is that traditional journalism will cede to such competitors both the new technology and the audience that is building there. For now, traditional media brands still control most of where audiences go online for news, but that is already beginning to change. In 2004, Google News emerged as a major new player in online news, and the audience for bloggers grew by 58% in six months, to 32 million people.
5. *The three broadcast network news divisions face their most important moment of transition in decades.* A generation of network journalists is retiring. Two of the three anchors are new. One network, CBS, has said it wants to rethink nightly news entirely. *Nightline*, one of the ornaments of American broadcast journalism, was fighting for its life. After years of

programming inertia and audience decline, network news finds itself at a crossroads. If the networks rethink nightly news, will they build on the programs' strengths—carefully written, taped, and edited storytelling—or cut costs and make the shows more unscripted, like cable interview programs? Will they try to find network evening news a better time slot, or begin to walk away from producing signature nightly newscasts altogether because of the programs' aging demographics? Will ABC try to save *Nightline* because it adds to the network's brand, or drop it because the company could make more money with a variety show? Students in high school should observe carefully the degree to which passion, inertia, or math drives the future of network news.

Student Assessment

When we measure and document the knowledge, skills, attitudes, and beliefs of our students, we are using the process of assessment. We often assess as we are teaching (observations, questionnaires, inventories, checklists, scales, logs, diaries, anecdotal records, samples of pupil work, group discussions, tests, quizzes, pop quizzes, etc.) and we call this *formative assessment* because it helps us "form" (or reform) our teaching. It tells us where the students are and where we need to go next. It is checking for understanding so that we know the next direction to take in our teaching. *Summative assessment*, on the other hand, occurs after we have taught, after we have checked for understanding, after we feel the students know the material. When we administer a test to see if students have mastered the material, we are using the process of summative assessment.

Rubrics

For both formative and summative testing, rubrics are excellent for helping us align our teaching objectives and our testing objectives. As a matter of fact, the grade-level expectations that we use as objectives when we are planning our lessons can also be used in rubrics for our criteria in testing. Rubrics are excellent templates that help us organize our testing into scoring guides and performance criteria. Rubrics help define important outcomes for students when making assessments and evaluations. Well-crafted rubrics help teachers define learning targets so that they can plan instruction more effectively, be more consistent in scoring student work, and be more systematic in reporting student progress.

Rubrics can generally be divided into holistic or analytical trait rubrics and must be of high quality in order to have positive effects in the classroom. The grade-level expectations (discussed at length in Section V) are excellent criteria for use in scoring rubrics, both holistic and analytic. An excellent Web site for learning how to make all sorts of rubrics for assessment purposes is

Kathy Schrock's *Guide for Educators: Assessment & Rubric Information* (http://school.discovery.com/schrockguide/assess.html#rubrics). Tables 6.2 and 6.3 are examples of an *analytic rubric* and a *holistic rubric*, respectively.

Table 6.2 Analytic Rubric

	Beginning (1)	Developing (2)	Accomplished (3)	Exemplary (4)	Score
Makes a papier mâché globe	The product reflects a beginning level of performance	The product reflects movement toward the mastery level of performance.	The product reflects achievement of the mastery level of performance.	The product reflects the highest level of performance.	
Labels political boundaries	The labels reflect a beginning level of performance.	The labels reflect movement toward the mastery level of performance.	The labels reflect achievement of the mastery level of performance.	The labels reflect the highest level of performance.	
Describes three critical movements	The description reflects a beginning level of performance.	The description reflects movement toward the mastery level of performance.	The description reflects achievement of the mastery level of performance.	The description reflects the highest level of performance.	

Table 6.3 Holistic Rubric

Score	Description
5	Demonstrates a complete understanding of the problem, and all requirements of the task are included in the response.
4	Demonstrates a considerable understanding of the problem, and all requirements of the task are included.
3	Demonstrates a partial understanding of the problem, and most requirements of the task are included.
2	Demonstrates little understanding of the problem; many requirements of the task are missing.
1	Demonstrates no understanding of the problem.
0	No response, or the task was not attempted.

Norm-Referenced and Criterion-Referenced Tests[6]

Assessment tests administered to students to determine how they perform in comparison to others are called *norm-referenced tests.* They are often used to classify students for placement and award purposes. One well-known example is the use of the PSAT test for determining participation in the National Merit Scholarship award program. A student's current test performance is compared to that of a representative sample of students, known as a norm group, who were previously administered the test. Norm groups can be used to create either national norms or local norms, depending on who is included in the normative sample.

Norm-referenced tests have several strengths. Norm-referenced testing often allows for reliable and objective measurement. However, with these types of assessments, it is critical to understand the composition of the norm group. It's also important to note that test scores on norm-referenced tests typically rise the longer the test is in use, likely due to changes in instruction or test preparation that are made as educators become more familiar with the form of a test.

Criterion-referenced tests are tests of mastery on specific content. A teacher-made test is a criterion-referenced test. Having taught the specific content, checked for understanding, and provided opportunities for practice, the

Criterion-referenced tests provide useful information about students' strengths and weaknesses in various curriculum areas.

teacher now creates a test to see if the student has mastered the material. The criterion is: Does the student know the material that was taught? Criterion-referenced and norm-referenced tests yield different, but complementary, pieces of information. Criterion-referenced tests, such as many of the state high school tests, help demonstrate how a student stands in relation to a given educational curriculum. The emphasis is not on comparison with other students, but rather on mastery of specific content knowledge and skills. Criterion-referenced tests provide useful information about students' strengths and weaknesses in various curriculum areas. It is critical that the content domain of the assessment be clearly defined. Results of norm- and criterion-referenced tests should be combined with other formal and informal data collection methods, since no single set of test scores is adequate to make important educational decisions.

National Testing[7]

The United States, unlike many other countries, has no national test that every student in every state takes to demonstrate mastery of some agreed-upon body of knowledge and skills. Commercial test publishers have long offered achievement tests (e.g., the Iowa Test of Basic Skills, the California Achievement Test, the Terra Nova) that are administered to schools across the country and normalized on national samples, but these are not in themselves national tests because individual schools, districts, or states decide for themselves whether to use them and which to select. The SAT is probably the most common test administered in the country, but it is intended to measure college-bound students' aptitude for college work, not academic achievement across a wide range of subjects for all students, and it has the ACT as competition.

The question of the appropriate role for the federal government to play in testing is a complicated one, and like many policy matters it has strong political overtones. Over the past two decades, many policy makers have moved from an initial position of strong support for some sort of a national test used as an accountability tool to opposition on the grounds that a national test would usher in a national curriculum and lead to further federal involvement in what has historically been a state and local matter. These policy makers want states to establish and administer their own standards and assessments without interference from Washington; they see federal involvement in testing as a sometimes unwelcome effort to dictate what is important for their students to learn.

On the other hand, some policy makers seem to be less troubled by an expanded federal role in testing, but more suspicious about whether nationwide testing would lead to genuine school improvement and higher student achievement or just sort out and penalize low-performing schools and their students, who are disproportionately low income and minority. They argue that until there is truly equal opportunity to learn for all students (with equal access to technology, highly qualified teachers, good facilities, and other learning inputs), testing is an empty exercise. Some policy makers also fear that poor test scores might fuel discontent with the public school system and lead to more support for controversial initiatives such as vouchers for private school aid.

Federally mandated testing also raises a variety of practical and technical questions, including the following:

- Who will pay the considerable cost of developing and administering additional tests?
- Do states have the technical expertise and personnel to conduct another large-scale assessment and analyze and report results?
- Will the tests be valid, and will scores be reliable for high-stakes purposes such as making decisions about which schools receive financial incentives and which are sanctioned for low performance?
- How will existing state tests be linked to each other, or to "yardsticks" such as NAEP or commercial tests, so that student and school progress can be measured fairly and accurately, particularly if rewards and sanctions are tied to results?

The National Assessment of Educational Progress, nicknamed "the nation's report card," is a congressionally mandated project of the National Center for Education Statistics (NCES) within the U.S. Department of Education. The NAEP assessment is administered annually by NCES to a nationally representative sample of public and private school students in grades 4, 8, and 12 to get a picture of what American children know and can do. NAEP results are usually watched closely because the assessment is considered a highly respected, technically sound longitudinal measure of U.S. student achievement. Two subject areas are typically assessed each year. Reading, mathematics, writing, and science are assessed most frequently, usually at four-year intervals so that trends can be monitored. Civics, U.S. history, geography, and the arts have also been assessed in recent years, and foreign language was assessed for the first time in 2003. Once exclusively multiple choice, NAEP now includes performance-based items that call for students to work with science kits, use calculators, prepare writing samples, and create art projects.

Students in participating schools are randomly selected to take one portion of the assessment being administered in a given year (usually administered during a 1½ to 2-hour testing period). Achievement is reported at one of three levels: *basic*, for partial mastery; *proficient*, for solid academic performance; and *advanced*, for superior work. A forth level, *below basic*, indicates less-than-acceptable performance. Individual student, school, and district data are not reported. To help states measure students' academic performance over time and to allow for cross-state comparisons, a voluntary state component was added to NAEP in 1990. A 26-member independent board called the National Assessment Governing Board (NAGB) is responsible for setting NAEP policy, selecting which subject areas will be assessed, and overseeing the content and design of each NAEP assessment. NAGB does not attempt to specify a national curriculum but rather outlines what a national assessment should test, based on a national consensus process that involves gathering input from teachers, curriculum experts, policy makers, the business community, and the public.

While almost every state has implemented some sort of state testing program, the differences in what they measure, how they measure it, and how they set achievement levels make it virtually impossible to conduct meaningful state-by-state comparisons of individual student performance. Some people believe state-to-state comparisons are irrelevant because education is a state and local function. Others believe cross-state comparisons will help and are important to spur reform and ensure uniformly high-quality education across the country. Legislation being debated now calls for the use of NAEP or another nationally administered test as a check on the results of annual state tests. Theoretically, a state-level NAEP would yield useful data. In reality, however, NAEP state-level results have sometimes been confusing because achievement levels of students generally appear to be much lower on NAEP than on the state tests. This discrepancy may be attributed to a number of factors, including the following:

- State tests are more likely to be aligned with state curricula than NAEP is.
- State tests and NAEP use different definitions of proficiency.
- State tests and NAEP may use different formats.
- State tests and NAEP differ in terms of who takes them (e.g., whether students in special education or with limited English proficiency are included).

In general, fewer students are judged to reach the *proficient* standard on the NAEP reading and math tests than on state tests. This discrepancy can lead people who are not aware of the differences in the two types of tests to question the validity of their own state testing programs or the desirability of participating in a federal one. Using the results of any other nationally normalized standardized test poses the same difficulty.

It is difficult to predict how the national testing issue will ultimately be resolved. The federal government's plan calls for expanding testing in most states and gives NAEP and commercial tests a more prominent role than they currently have. Teachers might be torn between continuing to teach the curriculum aligned with their state assessment or switching gears to focus on whatever other test is being used to determine rewards and sanctions. Given the classroom implications of expanded testing, it makes sense for teachers to stay active in the discussion.

Performance Assessments[8]

As the term suggests, performance assessments require a demonstration of students' skills or knowledge. Performance assessments can take on many different forms, which include written and oral demonstrations and activities that can be completed by either a group or an individual. A factor that distinguishes performance assessments from other extended-response activities is that they require students to demonstrate the application of knowledge in a particular context. Through observation or analysis of a student's response, the teacher can determine what the student knows, what the student does not know, and what misconceptions the student holds with respect to the purpose of the assessment. Following are recommendations for developing performance assessments.

- The selected performance should reflect a valued activity. The best tests always teach students and teachers alike the kind of work that most matters; they are enabling and forward-looking, not just reflective of prior teaching. Tasks are best that resemble the type of activities that are known to take place in the workforce (e.g., project reports and presentations; writing legal briefs; collecting, analyzing, and using data to make and justify decisions). In other words, performance assessments allow students the opportunity to display their skills and knowledge in response to "real" situations.
- The completion of performance assessments should provide a valuable learning experience. Performance assessments require more time to administer than do other forms of assessment. The investment of this classroom time should result in a higher payoff. This payoff should include both an increase in the teacher's understanding of what students know and can do and an increase in the students' knowledge of the intended content and constructs.
- The statement of goals and objectives should be clearly aligned with the measurable outcomes of the performance activity. Once the task has been selected, a list can be made of how the elements of the task map into the desired goals and objectives. If it is not apparent as to how the students' performance will be mapped into the desired goals and objectives, then adjustments may need to be made to the task or a new task may need to be selected.
- The task should not examine extraneous or unintended variables. Examine the task and think about whether there are elements of the task that do not map directly into the goals and objectives. Is knowledge required in the completion of the task that is inconsistent with the purpose? Will lack of this knowledge interfere or prevent the students from completing the task for reasons that are not consistent with the task's purpose? If such factors exist, changes may need to be made to the task or a new task may need to be selected.
- Performance assessments should be fair and free from bias. The phrasing of the task should be carefully constructed in a manner that eliminates gender and ethnic stereotypes. Additionally, the task should not give an unfair advantage to a particular subset of students. For exam-

ple, a task that is heavily weighted with baseball statistics may give an unfair advantage to the students who are baseball enthusiasts.

Scoring rubrics are one method that may be used to evaluate students' responses to performance assessments. Two types of performance assessments are frequently discussed in the literature: analytic and holistic. Analytic scoring rubrics divide a performance into separate facets, and each facet is evaluated using a separate scale. Holistic scoring rubrics use a single scale to evaluate the larger process. In holistic scoring rubrics, all of the facets that make up the task are evaluated in combination.

The criteria set forth within a scoring rubric should be clearly aligned with the requirements of the task and the stated goals and objectives. A list can be compiled that describes how the elements of the task map into the goals and objectives.

Administering Performance Assessments. Once a performance assessment and its accompanying scoring rubric are developed, it is time to administer the assessment to students. The recommendations that follow are specifically developed to guide the administration process for performance assessments.

- Both written and oral explanations of tasks should be clear and concise and presented in language that the students understand. If the task is presented in written form, then the reading level of the students should be given careful consideration. Students should be given the opportunity to ask clarification questions before completing the task.
- Appropriate tools need to be available to support the completion of the assessment activity. Depending on the activity, students may need access to library resources, computer programs, laboratories, calculators, or other tools. Before the task is administered, the teacher should determine what tools will be needed and ensure that these tools are available during the task administration.
- Scoring rubrics should be discussed with the students before they complete the assessment activity. This allows the students to adjust their efforts in a manner that maximizes their performance. Teachers are often concerned that by giving the students the criteria in advance, all of the students will perform at the top level. In practice, this rarely (if ever) occurs.

Paper-and-Pencil Tests in the Classroom

As classroom teachers, we frequently give paper-and-pencil tests with either supply-type items (e.g., fill-in-the-blank, short answer, or essay questions) or selection-type items (e.g., true-false, multiple choice, or matching). Typically, supply-type items are very easy to score; they can even be administered on Scantron sheets and machine scored. Anyone with the scoring key can grade them. Supply-type items are another matter; they must be graded by you and only you. Scoring supply-type items is subjective and they should only be judged by your subjectivity. On the other hand, it is very easy to create supply-type items that penetrate the depths of higher-order thinking. For example, "List and describe the salient features leading up to Napoleon's exile." But the creation of selection-type items which examine higher-order thinking is more difficult. You must labor, sometimes at length, to get a selection-type item to get beyond simple factual recall. Also, selection-type items have to be carefully checked for accuracy. You must be very sure that your true-false questions have only one correct true/false answer. In the same way, your multiple choice and matching questions can have but one choice. If you err, you will always have students who will be eager to point out the flaws in your test!

Because your paper-and-pencil assessments yield scores, you can do a quick statistical procedure with your test scores to see whether your test was, statistically speaking, a good test. If the procedure gives three measures of central tendency (mean, median, and mode) that are close to the same, then the probability is that the test was a good test. But if any one of the three measures of central tendency is skewed apart from the others, the probability is that the test has flaws; best to revise it or throw it out and start over. Figure 6.3 shows the procedure for finding the three measures of central tendency for scores from your tests:

Figure 6.3 Mean, Median, Mode

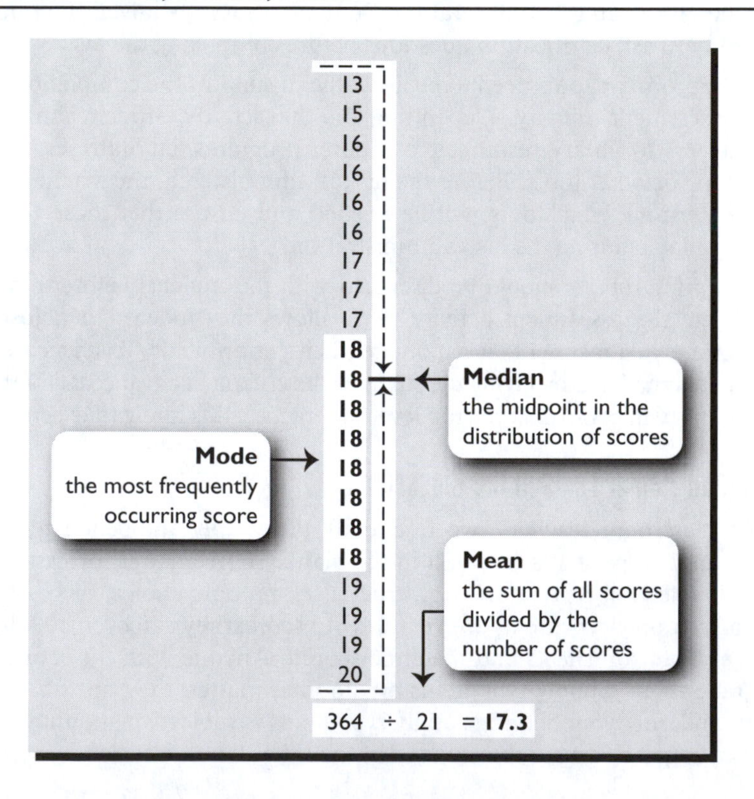

A Comment on Scoring. How should teachers respond when children make careless mistakes on a test? On one hand, teachers want students to learn to follow directions, to think through their work, to check their work, and to be careful. On the other hand, tests are supposed to reflect what a student knows. A low score due to careless mistakes is not the same as a low score due to lack of knowledge.

A bad test due to careless mistakes should not dramatically lower a student's grade for the semester. The semester grade should reflect what the student has achieved, since that is the meaning it will convey to others. It might be wise to keep two sets of records for some students who are prone to carelessness on tests. One set reflects production, and the other reflects achievement. The teacher then has the needed data to apply good judgment in conferencing with students and parents and for determining semester grades.

Notes

[1] Adapted from Thomas R. McDaniel (September, 1986), A primer on classroom discipline: Principles old and new, *Phi Delta Kappan 68* (1), 63–67; and a further adaptation by Budd Churchward (2003), *The Honor Level System: Discipline by Design.*

[2] Adapted from Schreyer Institute for Teaching Excellence (1992), *Teaching by discussion.*

[3] Adapted from Bonnie Potts (1994), *Strategies for Teaching Critical Thinking.* ERIC/AE Digest.

[4] Adapted from Linda Lumsden (Jul. 1997), *Expectations for Students* (ED409609). ERIC Digest.

[5] The Project for Excellence in Journalism, *The State of the News Media 2005: An Annual Report on American Journalism.* Used by permission.

[6] Adapted from David M. Monetti and Terry T. Hinkle, *Five Important Test Interpretation Skills for School Counselors* (ED481472 2003-09-00). ERIC Digest.

[7] Adapted from Carol Boston, *The Debate over National Testing* (ED458214 2001-04-00). ERIC Digest.

[8] Adapted from Barbara M. Moskal, *Developing Classroom Performance Assessments and Scoring* (ED481714 2003-06-00). ERIC Digest.

SECTION VII

Vital Topics and Critical Issues in Social Studies

Vital Topics in Social Studies

Vital topics in social studies are those contemporary social issues, social problems, and social challenges which are of exceptional importance to the society and which endure over long periods of time. They are topics which beg attention from social studies teachers and can't be ignored. From time to time, there will be differing opinions about which topics are vital and which are not, but the following topics are widely agreed upon as being of vital importance and worthy of consideration in today's social studies programs. The current eight vital topics appear in figure 7.1.

Figure 7.1 Vital Topics

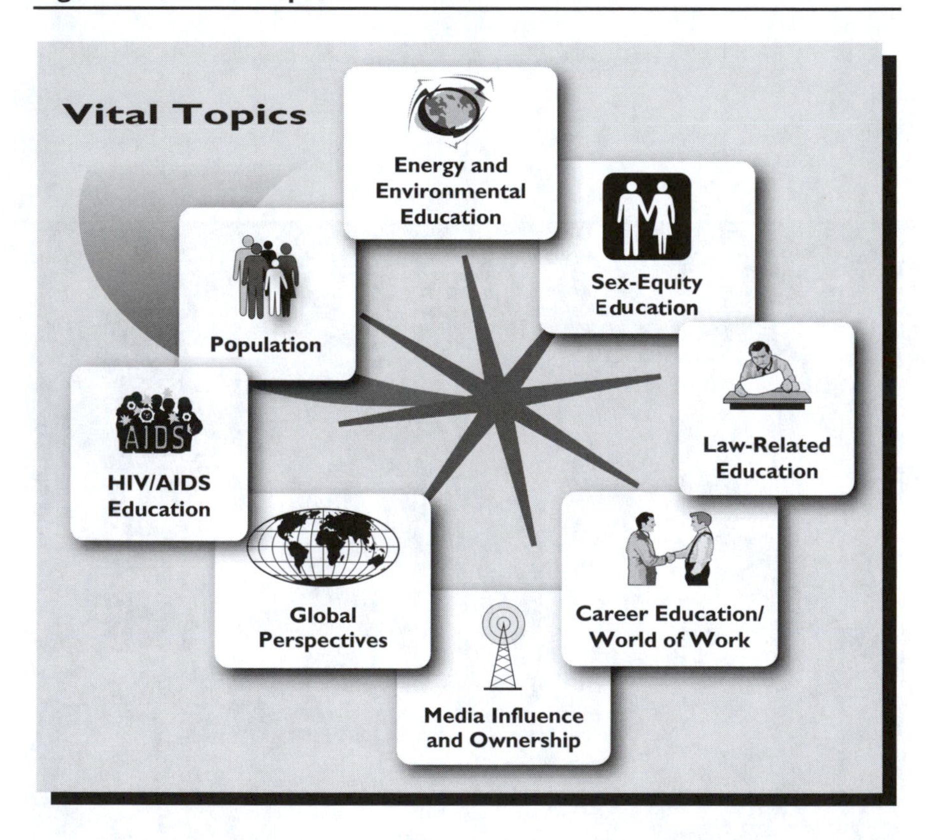

Energy and Environmental Education

Students easily relate to topics in energy and environment because they are a part of their daily lives. Energy is closely related to the day-to-day lives of most people. Extracting and consuming energy impacts the environment by scarring or polluting the Earth. Dangers to the environment stem from pesticides, solid waste disposal, air pollution, water pollution, radioactive substances, and overpopulation. The social studies teacher can lead the class in discussions about ways in which human activity might be harmful to the environment. Energy and environmental topics can often be taught in science and health education.

Concepts to teach: environment, ecosystem, balance of nature, population, adaptation, resources, energy, pollution, industrialization

Internet Resources for Environmental and Energy Education

- *North American Association for Environmental Education*
  Designed to support students, teachers and professionals who support K–12 environmental education. Features a Teacher Resources section with an abundant selection of classroom activities, lesson plans, and links to environmental education-related sites.
  http://eelink.net/pages/Site+Mapp+New#teach
- *U.S. Environmental Protection Agency—Environmental Education*
  The High School Environmental Center page features resources for air, waste and recycling, water, conservation, your neighborhood, ecosystems, and health and safety.
  http://www.epa.gov/highschool

  The Teaching Center page features curriculum resources (including lesson plans and activities), suggestions for community service projects, and links to other quality environmental education sites.
  http://www.epa.gov/teachers/
- *National Energy Education Development Project*
  This Web site features curriculum guides and activities, program implementation resources for teachers, an energy knowledge assessment tool, and curriculum correlations to both national and state standards.
  http://www.need.org/guides.htm

Law-Related Education

Fundamental constitutional and legal principles are central to effective and powerful instruction in the secondary social studies curriculum. To become competent citizens, students need to develop a rich understanding of the principles on which their society and government rest. Few principles are as important in the social studies curriculum as due process of law. It is important, then, to trace the history and development of due process of law, and to contrast procedural and substantive due process. The World Wide Web offers resources that are helpful in teaching and learning about due process of law.

Due process has become a defining feature of American constitutionalism and an inherent part of justice in the United States. Both procedural and substantive due process have been used to place constitutional limits on the powers of government, and to protect the rights of individuals against infringement by either federal or state government. Thus, due process of law, both procedural and substantive, is foundational to understanding the U.S. system of government. Teaching and learning about due process of law deserves a prominent place in the social studies curriculum, particularly in history, government, and civics classes.

Law-related education helps students develop an understanding of the legal system and the justice system. Young Americans need to realize that they are preserving civil rights and liberties by becoming responsible citizens. In the traditional social studies program, law-related education meant the study of the structure and processes of our government and the fundamental rights and responsibilities of citizens. While those elements are still present, today's program extends to the real issues and problems of the streets; to everyday, contemporary situations.

Through role playing, case studies, simulations, and mock trials, students can examine the roles of police, jails, judges, bailiffs, court reporters, prosecutors, defense counsels, public defenders, probation officers, social workers, and others. Children's literature, too, provides abundant opportunities to engage in law-related education. Local attorneys who belong to the American Bar Association are excellent resource persons, as are local politicians.

Concepts to teach: rules, laws, due process, authority, power, rights, justice, privacy, property, responsibility, equal protection, legal system

Internet Resources for Law-Related Education

- *U.S. Constitution Online*
  A comprehensive Web site about all aspects of the United States Constitution. Students and teachers will find detailed information about the history and interpretation of the due process clauses of the Fifth and Fourteenth Amendments.
  http://www.usconstitution.net/index.html
- *FindLaw*
  Although designed for use by legal professionals, this Web site may be used by students or teachers to obtain detailed information about the

Supreme Court's interpretation of the due process clauses of the Fifth and Fourteenth Amendments to the United States Constitution.
http://www.findlaw.com/

- *The Bill of Rights and the Fourteenth Amendment*
This Web site is an excellent resource for teachers and students who want to learn more about incorporation of the Bill of Rights. The site contains an extensive analysis of the incorporation doctrine by a leading legal theorist, Akhil Reed Amar of Yale Law School.
http://www.saf.org/LawReviews/Amar1.html

Media Influence and Ownership

The media encompass all of the mass communication vehicles, such as newspapers, magazines, periodicals, trade books, textbooks, radio, television, and the Internet, and they are singularly influential in our lives. The media are all-powerful in how we conceptualize and view the world. There is evidence that ownership sometimes intrudes into the editorial policies of segments of the media delivery system. By and large, ownership should not interfere with the editorial policies of various kinds of media, especially those who report the news.

A second concern regarding the media has arisen over the violence of its content. Heavy exposure to televised violence is one of the causes of aggressive behavior, crime, and violence in society. Parents can be effective in reducing the negative effects of viewing television. A ratings system has been developed by the television industry in collaboration with child advocacy organizations to assist parents in determining what they consider appropriate for their children to watch.

The Federal Communications Commission (FCC), established in 1934, is an independent government agency responsible for regulating U.S. radio, television, satellite, and cable broadcasting. Traditionally, the FCC has traditionally sought to prevent the emergence of dominant media monopolies by establishing limits on media ownership. Many people agree that by opening the door to more media and newspaper consolidation, the FCC has endangered something that reaches far beyond traditional politics: It has undermined the community-oriented communications critical to our democracy. Conservatives see a link between the growth of big media and the amount of blood and skin they see on television. The smaller and more localized the media, the argument goes, the more attuned to community standards of decency. If local stations could preempt what was being fed from New York and Los Angeles, then programming could be more reflective of family values. Here again, the sense is that media have become too large and all-encompassing and lost touch with their audience.

Concepts to teach: manipulation, hype, sensationalism, exploitation, ratings, censorship, infotainment

Internet Resources for Teaching about the Media

- *Columbia Review: Who Owns What?*
  Ownership of huge media holdings is dwindling into the hands of a few. Search *CJR*'s online guide to what major media companies own. Also offered are links to a selected list of *CJR* articles about media ownership.
  http://www.cjr.org/tools/owners/
- *The State of the News Media 2005: An Annual Report on American*
  With the growing consolidation of already large media corporations, pressure on journalists for biased coverage might be increasing. This report analyzes significant differences in the nature of content of, and the nature of reporting in, different media.
  http://www.stateofthemedia.com/2005/narrative_overview_intro.asp?cat=1&media=1

HIV/AIDS Education

Acquired Immune Deficiency Syndrome (AIDS) is characterized by a loss of immunity to infection. AIDS allows treatable illnesses and infections, like tuberculosis or a throat infection, to become unmanageable and fatal. While in most cases the two terms HIV and AIDS are used together, they actually mean two different things. AIDS is a term used to refer to several different illnesses that someone may contract after she or he has been infected with the human immunodeficiency virus (HIV). Inside the body of an HIV-infected person, this virus slowly destroys the body's defenses for fighting off diseases. After some time, the person infected with HIV will begin to contract serious illnesses. At this point, the person will be diagnosed as having AIDS—that is, to be suffering from AIDS-related illnesses. There is no cure for AIDS, and after some years, the infected person will die. Because of the sexual nature of HIV transmission, experts have emphasized that AIDS education must be given to young people before they first engage in sexual activity.

Students with AIDS have the most difficult tasks, not only of dealing with a painful and probably fatal illness but also of fighting for love and acceptance from the people around them.

Concepts to teach: human immunodeficiency virus (HIV), acquired immune deficiency syndrome (AIDS), virus, epidemic, infectious disease, contagion

Internet Resources for HIV/AIDS Education

- *AIDS Education Global Information System*
  http://www.aegis.com/

- *AVERT—HIV/AIDS and Sex Education*
  http://www.avert.org/educate.htm
- *AIDS Education & Training Centers National Resource Center*
  http://www.aids-ed.org/
- *American Red Cross Health & Safety Services, HIV/AIDs Programs*
  http://www.redcross.org/services/hss/hivaids/
- *Teenage AIDS Education*
  http://library.thinkquest.org/10631/menu.htm
- *U.S. Department of Health & Human Services, AIDSinfo*
  http://www.aidsinfo.nih.gov/
- *The Centers for Disease Control (CDC)*
  http://www.cdc.gov/

  CDC National Prevention Information Network (NPIN)
  http://www.cdcnpin.org/scripts/hiv/index.asp

  Call 1-800-458-5231 (M–F 9 AM–8 PM ET), or e-mail info@cdcnpin.org for up-to-the-minute educational information about AIDS.

Population

Over the last few centuries, the world's population has grown dramatically. In 1700, just over 300 years ago, the world's population was 400 million. In 1880, the population of the world had grown to 1 billion. In 1950, it was 3 billion. Today, the population of the world is 6 billion people! The most populated regions of the world are East Asia (China and Japan; 1.5 billion), South Asia (India; 1 billion), and Indonesia (Java and surrounding areas; 2 billion). Some 4.5 billion people live in these areas. In Egypt and Iran, two of the largest countries in the Middle East, the population doubled over the last 30 years.

Dramatic growth in world population is due to a number of factors. People are living longer lives in some areas due to better dietary habits, better health care, and new medicines. People have less risk of dying young because of immunizations and preventive measures that were unavailable a century ago.

The birthrate is lowest in the United States, Northern Europe, and Japan (2 per mother), but life expectancy is longer (about 70+ years), so population is becoming older. The birthrate is highest in Africa (5 per mother), but life expectancy is short (about 50 years), so population in Africa is becoming younger.

Giant cities are emerging, with growth rates faster than those of the countries in which they are found. Housing and providing basic services like water, electricity, and garbage and sewage disposal is the biggest problem in these giant cities. Mexico City (now the largest city in the world with 20+ million people), Cairo (11+ million), and Bangkok (8+ million) are examples of giant cities.

Concepts to teach: immigration, birthrate, overpopulated, emigrate, population stabilization, zero growth-level birthrate, preventive measures, immunization.

Internet Resources on Population

- *Population Reference Bureau—Educators Forum*
  ". . . informs people around the world about population, health, and the environment, and empowers them to use that information to advance the well-being of current and future generations." Features lesson plans, classroom activities, and links to other useful Web sites.
  http://www.prb.org/template.cfm?Section=Educators
- *Facing the Future: People and the Planet*
  Features information on global population and sustainability; includes a Teachers Corner with curricula, activities and lesson plans, and a "Facing the Future" newsletter.
  http://www.teacherscorner.org/newsletter.html
- *World Population Clock*
  Visitors to this Web page can watch the current population as it changes from second to second and can compare it to population data from years past.
  http://www.ibiblio.org/lunarbin/worldpop
- *U.S. Census Bureau—Special Topics for Teachers*
  In addition to the useful data featured on the Bureau's home page, visitors to this URL will find a Census in Schools program overview and highlights, teaching/learning materials, downloadable reference materials, and more.
  http://www.census.gov/dmd/www/teachers.html

Global Perspectives

World-mindedness will continue to grow on Earth. Isolationism is no longer a viable policy, and global perspectives have become important. Not only do modern systems of production and distribution have little regard for national boundaries; Americans visiting older countries in Europe are likely to find American popular music rather than the traditional folk music of the country—illustrating that culture, too, now transcends national boundaries. Today, what happens in the smallest of nations can have the potential to impact everyone on Earth (for example, a minor power armed with modern weapons could be a threat to the entire world). We must deal with the world the way it is, not the way we wish it to be. Students, then, should be alerted to the realities of life on Earth.

Global perspectives education need not be an addition to the curriculum. It can occur through experiences in art, music, science, literature, reading, and the like. Global perspectives education often focuses on specific nations. Students learn information about a nation's geography, economics, and politics, and how nations join together to form power blocs.

Teaching about the United Nations can be controversial in some communities; learn about the community and use good judgment. Multi-ethnic education has as its goal the improvement of the quality of human relations. Build social cohesiveness by helping students gain an understanding of the diversity of people.

Concepts to teach: cross-cultural, transnational, globalization, global system, conflict, communication, interdependence, third-world nations, developed nations, developing nations, culture, ethnicity, ethnocentrism, pluralism, heritage, race, stereotype, assimilation, status, discrimination, prejudice, social protest

Sex Equity Education

One of the most significant social developments of our time has been, and is, the increasing independence of women, primarily in America but also to some extent in other parts of the world. Sex discrimination is expressly forbidden by legislation in the United States (the best-known legislation being the Nineteenth Amendment, the Civil Rights Act of 1964, and Title IX of Education Amendments of 1972). Sex equity education is that part of the instructional program dealing with gender issues, particularly sex-role stereotyping. Social studies programs have a responsibility to teach the inequities of sex-role stereotyping through a program of sex-equity education that includes awareness of and practices that exclude sexist language, attitudes, and behaviors. Because sex equity instruction must cut across all curricular lines, it is ideally suited for an interdisciplinary approach to teaching in the social studies.

Concepts to teach: gender equity, sex roles, sexist language, reform movements, equality of opportunity, nontraditional roles

Career Education/The World of Work

Good adult citizens need to be self supporting, usually through some form of occupation—employment, line of work, business, job, trade, vocation—an activity that serves as one's regular source of livelihood; a career. Thus the rationale for *career education*, the term used to describe the school's efforts to teach about the world of work, which has long been a topic in school social studies classes. Community helpers and community workers often are topics for units. Helping students develop career awareness and explore a broad spectrum of occupations and careers is the focal point of career education in the school.

Concepts to teach: career, career families, work, leisure, lifestyle, occupation, interests, values

Critical Issues in Social Studies

Although issues like diversity and technology are not "vital topics" for students, per se, they certainly are vital considerations for teachers. Among the most critical issues confronting the social studies teacher are diversity, multicultural education, inclusive education, character education, and technology.

Diversity

Diversity is recognizing the reality of difference. Dimensions of difference may include ethnicity and race (such as indigenous, immigrant, and minority), gender (including sexual orientation), socioeconomic status, locale (global and regional locations) and (dis)ability. Being aware, cognizant, and understanding of diversity is increasingly important in this age of globalization.

There is no place on Earth that cannot be reached in person by modern transportation, through modern communications, via modern media, or through products and services via modern markets. And because they *can* be reached, almost invariably they *will* be reached. Look, for example, at the area of commerce and economics where production, distribution, and consumption increasingly defy national borders and utilize diverse labor forces as they strive to take their exchange to the ends of the Earth. In the realm of governance, a kind of "civic pluralism" is developing as nations, states, and local communities negotiate differences resulting from immigration, refugee movements, sovereignty, and indigenous claims, as well as a plethora of other intersecting and often contrary differences. Diversity in the world is causing humankind to take a new look at human rights.

Differences sit deeply within our personalities, as well. Our epistemologies and our subjectivities are affected by this bit of race, that bit of gender, this area of socioeconomic status, and so on, until the resultant complexities are enormous.

The social studies classroom becomes a place for thinking about, speaking about, and exploring the pressing matters of difference and diversity. Our classroom activities in this arena should take us from the theoretical to the very practical aspects of negotiating difference and diversity in our real, everyday lives.

Multicultural Education

Recognizing the reality of difference is directly linked to *multicultural education.*[1] Youth from culturally diverse backgrounds often face contrasting notions of self because they must function in schools and educational systems that are organized around the values and goals of the *dominant culture,* that of the people who either are the greatest in number or have the most political and economic power. In the United States, the dominant culture has been defined by white European Americans, specifically those very few who have a great amount of power and wealth. Students who are not from the dominant culture may be victim to unspoken yet powerful stereotypes and messages about their development and personal identity. Hence, they must learn to negotiate and bridge multiple, and often competing, identities in the schools.

Racial and ethnic minority students must learn to operate successfully in the dominant—white—system since they are evaluated based on its norms. This means that students are expected to develop a sense of autonomy and self-reliance and to accept that the individual is seen as the fundamental, or most important, unit of society. Such understanding of the self as unique has clear implications for how students are treated in school. Generally speaking, students from collectivistic cultures (as opposed to those from individualistic cultures, for example) must learn to be assertive, independent, and confident to succeed in schools, but they must also be able to shift back to being relational, modest, passive, and family-oriented in at home. Moreover, home and school contexts are only two of the multiple settings in which students learn to operate across cultures. They must also learn to shift and adapt to culture-based role expectation of peers, elders, and significant others. Those who are unable to adapt to such competing and fluid role demands are often alienated from society.

Students from diverse cultural backgrounds learn to adapt to Western cultural norms in the school context in many ways. For example, teachers help them identify internal, personal attributes that make each student different and independent from another. They emphasize positive attributes in students (intelligence, control, maturity, and success) in order to build self-esteem. Teachers also help orient students to the future by asking them to consider the questions of what will be, or what they could become (future self). This developed sense of individuality, uniqueness, and freedom of choice can be seen in children as early as preschool.

Minority-group students have more difficulty internalizing these aspects of the dominant culture. They show poorer school achievement and have substantially higher dropout rates than majority students, at least in part because of the incongruent expectations, motives, social behaviors, language, and cognitive patterns that teachers and majority students may have.

Non-Western cultures may be characterized by a strong orientation to family and community. Motivation for achievement may come from a desire to gain access to others and to maintain affiliative ties with peers rather than from a desire to attain personal or individual goals. To negotiate competing cultural norms and values, students must learn to be biculturally competent—that is, they must integrate two cultures without feeling the tension between the two. In establishing *bicultural competence*, individuals can adapt their behavior to a given social or cultural context without having to commit to a specific cultural identity. The ability to adjust across contexts and situations may include using different languages, as well as different problem-solving, coping, interpersonal, communication, and motivational styles of interaction.

Teachers can integrate this orientation into the curriculum by introducing more team and collaborative and cooperative approaches in the classroom so that students can work together and receive group rewards. Students might be given rewards that enable them to socialize with their peers, or an individualized activity can be paired with a group reward.

Cultural Influence and Identity. Minority cultural values and beliefs; differences in behaviors, language, and worldview; and past power experiences with the dominant culture all influence the success or failure in negotiating identities. For example, how discrepancies in one's sense of self are understood by minority individuals and what is seen as "normal" by the dominant culture may be quite different. The implications of this narrow view of "normality" are that minority individuals are often dismissed or pathologized in comparison to white school students, who are given more long-term support and guidance in schools.

Further, the way that students' "adjustment"—how they bridge competing identities across settings and contexts—is evaluated in the schools may predetermine an erroneous negative assessment. For example, students may have identity conflicts and question the essence of who they are at school, but function appropriately and effectively at home (or vice versa). To help students make a positive social and cultural adjustment, school professionals need an understanding of the students' cultural influences and of the many ways that social and emotional problems which emerge in school are perceived, evaluated, and treated around the world. Teachers should know the various ways that help is sought when a problem arises within the family. While students may need help in negotiating their identity or in dealing with other problems, it is not usual for them to seek support services independently if they are referred by teachers and parents.

School personnel must recognize the level of ethnocentrism that influences their evaluation of students. They must facilitate positive change in a child in ways that do not involve stereotyping, overgeneralizing, or pathologizing behavior that is inconsistent with the sanctioned dominant culture. They also need to realize that because ethnic minority youth must negotiate multiple identities, their youth selves are shifting and fluid, rather than static across home and school settings. Finally, all school personnel must recognize that culture may impact learning style, and consider the social context in which the child is observed, rather than trying to understand behaviors as unequivocal indicators of a student's individual personality or character.

A comprehensive multicultural education curriculum can provide students with rich and broad-based knowledge of the subjects covered, foster their understanding and appreciation of ethnic diversity, and promote positive interethnic relations. Multicultural educators need to tailor their curriculum to the developmental level and interests of students and to understand the different needs of majority and minority students. For example, in early childhood young children have concrete thinking processes and require experiential learning. Therefore, teachers can help them have personal experiences with other groups, share foods, and learn about different customs and holidays. Adolescents, with abstract thinking skills, can understand diversity through film, literature, and television and can assess how these media contribute to stereotyping, prejudice, and discrimination.

Majority students are more likely to be ethnocentric and less aware of ethnic differences. They need more accurate information about other groups and an understanding of the value of diversity in enriching a society. Minority students are typically already familiar with the majority culture, while their own culture has been ignored or disparaged by the curriculum. A better understanding (and acknowledgment by the school) of the strengths and achievements of their own culture will increase their self-esteem.

Negotiating multiple, often contradictory, identities is a complex process for culturally diverse school-age children. Social, cultural, and political factors unique to their backgrounds influence the process of identity development and the extent to which youth relate to values of the dominant and family cultures. Since identities are not solely dichotomous—home versus school—students may choose to embrace multiple ethnicities (identities) or may find safety in forming a cohesive self. Educators, therefore, should not normalize and pressure children to find a single identity. Rather, they need to acknowledge and accept multiple identities in students without prioritizing one over the other, and encourage students to appreciate their own cultural heritage and norms.

Internet Resources for Multicultural Education

- *Center for Multicultural Education*
  ". . . focuses on research projects and activities designed to improve practice related to equity issues, intergroup relations, and the achievement of all students. The Center also engages in services and teaching related to its research mission."
  http://depts.washington.edu/centerme/home.htm
- *National Association for Multicultural Education*
  An organization devoted to bringing together individuals and groups with an interest in multicultural education from all levels of education, different academic disciplines, and diverse educational institutions and occupations. Home of the journal *Multicultural Perspectives.*
  http://www.nameorg.org/
- *Multicultural Education Pavilion*
  Features links to Web sites on equity and diversity in education, curriculum reform, training and workshops, and a multicultural education listserv.
  http://www.edchange.org.multicultural/
- *Democracy and Diversity:*
  Principles and Concepts for Educating Citizens in a Global World
  Visit this Web site sponsored by the Center for Multicultural Educa-

tion for a free PDF download of this 2005 publication, which is "the product of a two-year project, supported by the Spencer Foundation and the University of Washington, that identified four important principles and ten concepts that constitute essential elements of effective citizenship education programs in democratic multicultural nation-states. It also contains a checklist designed to be used by educators who want to determine the extent to which these principles and concepts are reflected in their classrooms and schools."
http://depts.washington.edu/centerme/demdiv.htm

Inclusive Education

Recognizing the reality of difference also involves *inclusive education.* Schools with successful inclusion programs have faculties that work together. It is recognized that all teachers are specialists who bring their areas of expertise to the table when planning and making decisions about students. Classroom teachers are specialists in curriculum; special education teachers, including related service personnel, are specialists in the unique learning and behavior needs of students. Each specialist learns skills from the others with all students being the ultimate beneficiaries. Effectively bringing all of this expertise to the classroom requires adhering to organizational principles designed to help all students learn, yet allowing for their individual variations.

Classroom instruction should be tied to state and district curriculum standards and objectives, which should at some level be appropriate for all students. The following teaching strategies help students learn the curriculum and develop independent learning skills:

- Making accommodations and modifications for individuals when needed,
- Using multiple instructional delivery systems (e.g., visual, audio, multisensory),
- Using grouping variations such as cooperative learning groups,
- Helping students understand their own learning profiles, and
- Teaching them to use cognitive and metacognitive strategies.

Inclusive teaching also relies on ongoing informal classroom assessments so that teachers can begin teaching at the student's present performance level, keep abreast of student progress, and make appropriate instructional decisions. Assessments are matched to student learning styles. As classrooms are becoming more diverse, new instructional strategies and technologies are being developed to help teachers accommodate diversity. For example, principles of differentiation are being implemented and universal design is being applied to facilitate access to the curriculum by students of diverse abilities and needs. New directions such as these help all students move toward progress in the general curriculum. The partnerships which develop between regular classroom teachers and special education teachers will be crucial in determining the success of inclusion practices.

Individuals with Disabilities Education Act.[2] A new goal is challenging teachers: All students, with or without disabilities, including English language learners and students who are "falling between the cracks," are to achieve in the general education curriculum. For students with disabilities, access to the general education curriculum is mandated by the Individuals with Disabilities Education Act Amendments of 1997 (IDEA '97). Successful student access to the curriculum comes about through the implementation of validated programs and procedures. It calls for a paradigm shift that is required in the law: the student (if appropriate), special and general education teachers, parents, a district representative, and representatives of other agencies necessary to best serve the student's needs are required to take part in the student's educational planning, with improved learning in the general education curriculum as a goal.

Attitudes and Belief Systems. Improved student learning requires teachers, schools, and districts to give up unproductive traditions and beliefs, replacing them with validated practices and a full understanding of the intent of the law. Successful student access to the general education curriculum is most likely when there is general acceptance of the following principles:

- Responsibility for the learning outcomes of special education students is equally shared by the classroom teacher and the special education teacher.
- The classroom teacher is not only aware of the student's individual education plan (IEP) goals, but plays a significant role in determining those goals and providing instruction to help the student reach them.
- The classroom teacher is concerned with each student's strengths and needs.
- Administrators understand that teachers need time within their contracts to prepare standards-based activities and materials designed to meet the diverse needs of their students.
- Collaboration is valued. Time is allocated for teachers to collaborate with other teachers and parents regarding students. Ideally, paid days at the end of each school year are provided so that teachers can discuss their students, improving the students' chances for smooth transitions to the next grade.
- Expectations are not set according to a student's classification; it is recognized that a classification does not determine how much or how well the student will learn or perform.
- It is understood that good instruction incorporates variation in delivery, activities, expectations, and assessment to accommodate diverse learning strengths and needs.
- Accountability is considered a challenge, not a threat. As required by IDEA '97, students with disabilities are included in state and district assessments.
- Parents are considered to be a valuable part of the team.

Parent Involvement. IDEA '97 mandates that parents be participants in the educational planning for their children. These mandates support the idea that an inclusive school creates a society of learners that involves parents and the school's community in meaningful contributions to the education of its students. The following activities lead to productive collaboration between the parent and the school:

- Obtain information from parents about their child at the beginning of the year.
- Contact parents often, informing them of successes as well as problems.
- Contact parents at early onset of a learning or behavior problem, and ask them for feedback and ideas on how the problem could best be handled.
- As mandated in IDEA, invite the parents to any formal meetings concerning the student.

Transfer and Professional Development. IDEA '97 made federal funds available for in-service and pre-service training to states that qualify for a State Improvement Grant (SIG). These grants are awarded to states that have developed a plan to improve educational outcomes for students with disabilities.

Ensuring that all students gain access to the general education curriculum not only requires teacher commitment, but necessitates that districts support individual schools' efforts to improve teacher skills. Each school has its own set of unique circumstances. When staff identify and address their own training needs, they become better able to tackle the challenges they face in the classroom. In accordance with the principles of inclusion, a growing number of schools are assuming greater control over professional development activities, often moving from traditional training models to more participatory or job-embedded forms of learning.

Gaining District and Informed Legislative Support. State legislators need relevant and accurate information for making appropriate decisions regarding education statutes and funding. For example, implementing change usually requires additional teacher time and resources. In some states, legislatures and districts are allocating monies to provide for additional teacher-paid training days. States are also considering the idea of offering teachers varied contract options. For example, teachers interested in developing instructional plans and activities would be on an eleven-month contract, using non-teaching days to accomplish this. Their products would address the state curriculum standards as well as the diverse instructional and assessment needs of students. Through these efforts, databanks of curricular plans, activities, suggested materials, and additional resources can be made available online as well as in print.

Internet Resources for Inclusive Education

- *Inclusion*
  Sponsored by the University of Northern Iowa Department of Special Education/Renaissance Group, this Web site features teaching strategies, teacher competencies, inclusion resources, how to prepare for inclusion, and a multitude of other topics.
  http://www.uni.edu/coe/inclusion/
- *Council for Exceptional Children*
  ". . . dedicated to improving educational outcomes for individuals with exceptionalities, students with disabilities, and/or the gifted." Features a Teaching & Learning Center that includes current special education topics, instructional strategies, professional standards, and much more.
  http://www.cec.sped.org/

Character Education

Character education is reemerging as one of the fastest growing reform movements in education today. *Character education* is viewed as any deliberate approach by which school personnel, often in conjunction with parents and community members, help children and youth become caring, principled, and responsible citizens of the society. All pre-service and in-service teachers need to be cognizant of and informed about various Pre-K–12 character education programs. Currently, nearly every state mandates some aspect of character education curricula in their schools. Generally, classroom teachers work along with school counselors in introducing and administering character education programs in their schools.

Character education is based on the premise that teaching for character is essential for the success of a democratic society. A democratic society is based on the ideals of respect for others, regard for fairness and justice, concern for the common good, and voluntary participation in helping others. Many educators who implement character education in their schools believe that it helps students develop ethically, socially, and academically and helps them better understand their personal and community responsibility.

Character education is an inclusive concept regarding all aspects of how schools can support the positive character development of students. *Character* includes the emotional, intellectual, and moral qualities of a person or group, as well as the demonstration of these virtues in pro-social behavior and a moral life. Relevant virtues include honesty, justice and fairness, trustworthiness, responsibility, respect, altruism, generosity, patience, perseverance, appreciation of diversity, and courage. The development of related skills such as moral reasoning, problem solving, interpersonal skills, work ethic, empathy, and self-reflection are recognized as essential for optimal character development. The social environment of the school is also recognized as essential to character development (leadership, collegiality, and a learning orientation among faculty; and ties among school, home, and community). In a reciprocal fashion, practicing the virtues of civic engagement, civility, and citizenship and embracing the values of democracy are recognized as necessary for both the student and the community.

Divergent Points of View.[3] According to Evelyn Holt Otten (2000), the inclusion of character education is often a thorny issue for schools. Critics raise questions about "whose values" are to be taught. Some critics consider character education to be indoctrination in values contrary to those taught at home. If the selected values, however, are outcomes of decisions involving all stakeholders in the school community, then they should not conflict with those taught at home. Another criticism is that character education has no "substantive" quality and does little to improve scores on standardized tests. How do we know if it is working? What about performance on those high-stakes tests? Many schools with successful character education programs have observed not only higher performance scores on standardized achievement tests, but also fewer disciplinary referrals for misbehavior, improved school attendance, and fewer student dropouts. If schools become welcoming, supportive places for students, students are more likely to attend and stay on task. Student achievement is likely to improve.

Character education has long been a part of the educational scene, but interest in it is reemerging in light of apparent increases in disaffected students in school, school violence, voter apathy, declining test scores, and disinterest in community involvement. Character education integrated into the school community is a strategy to help re-engage our students, deal with conflict, keep students on task in the learning environment, and reinvest the community with active participation by citizens in political and civic life. Social studies teachers can be an integral part of establishing, creating, and maintaining viable and worthwhile character education programs in their high schools.

Internet Resources for Character Education

Numerous programs exist for character education. These models offer a variety of approaches that may be modified for the local school community. The following URLS feature a sampling of worthy programs.

goodcharacter.com (http://www.goodcharacter.com/HStopics.html) offers discussion questions, writing assignments, and student activities for character education. Among the featured topics on this Web site of teaching guides for high schools are trustworthiness, respect, responsibility, fairness/justice, caring, citizenship, honesty, courage, diligence, integrity, and school-to-work: ethics in the workplace.

Character Counts! (www.charactercounts.org) is a voluntary partnership which supports character education nationally. The six pillars of character identified by the coalition include respect, responsibility, trustworthiness, caring, fairness, and citizenship. A variety of resource materials are available, along with training sessions and awards recognition.

The Giraffe Project (www.giraffe.org) challenges participants to "stick their necks out" for good character. The program offers examples of heroes who "stuck their necks out" for the care and concern of others. Students explore the difference between "hero" and "celebrity" and work toward developing a caring local community. Resource materials are available for students in K–12.

The Character Education Partnership (www.character.org) was founded in 1993 as a national nonpartisan coalition for character education. The CEP recognizes National Schools of Character which serve as models of exemplary character education practice in the country.

Corporation for National Service (www.cns.gov), which was created under the National Community Service Trust Act in 1993, funds service learning projects in several states. *Service learning* is a vehicle for character education that actively involves students in addressing real community needs while maintaining direct academic ties with the classroom. Service learning is mandated in some states for high school graduation and is optional in others.

Technology

Technological literacy is an essential skill for every student in the increasingly technology-driven twenty-first century. Social studies is one of the school subjects that perhaps profits the most from the advancements that technology presents on an almost daily basis.

Internet Resources for Technological Literacy

- *International Society for Technology in Education*
  ". . . dedicated to providing leadership and service to improve teaching and learning by advancing the effective use of technology in K–12 education and teacher education." Home of the National Educational Technology Standards and the Center for Applied Research in Education Technology.
  http://www.iste.org/
- *Office of Educational Technology (OET)*
  The purpose of this U.S. Department of Education Web site "is to maximize technology's contribution to improving education. OET develops national educational technology policy and implements that policy department-wide, supporting the goals of No Child Left Behind and other initiatives."
  http://www.ed.gov/about/offices/list/os/technology/index.html

Political Cartoons. The technology of the Internet has made accessible one of the most valuable teaching tools for social studies in the form of scores of political cartoons from all over the world, available on a daily basis. Stu-

The ability to find information is the crux of technological literacy for students in secondary schools.

dents can work independently, in pairs, or in small groups to find cartoons which provide an array of topics for discussion, debate, and research. The cartoons are highly motivational, and students are quickly thrust into opportunities for developing and exercising higher-order thinking skills. An excellent place to begin the use of political cartoons in the classroom is the Cagle Web site (http://www.cagle.com/main.asp), which not only provides an extensive array of cartoons from throughout the United States and the world but also provides lesson plans for teachers to use in teaching with the cartoons.

Digitized Images. We often hear that a picture is worth a thousand words. But when it comes to teaching, it's quite possible that pictures, drawings, images, and graphics may be worth even more. They provide excellent tools for launching instruction. Once again, the Internet has opened the door for us. Are you planning to talk about river systems in class? With pictures and images obtained from the Internet, you can show rivers and river systems from all over the world; even graphic simulations of how rivers carry silt and drop them as sediments as they arrive at their destinations. United Streaming (http://www.unitedstreaming.com) has taken it a step farther, providing an extensive array of online videos about every topic under the sun. As with all searches, www.google.com is an excellent place to look for images, too. Just click on "images" in the Google toolbar before engaging in your search and the search engine will find myriad pictures, drawings, and graphics on your topic. Another good starting place is the digital picture and source document library of the Louisiana Digital Library collection (http://louisdl.louislibraries.org/). Photographs and images are great "take-off points" for highly motivational teaching and learning episodes.

Electronic Newspapers and Magazines. Keeping up to date, engaging in current events discussions, and conducting collaborative studies about the media's ethics and honesty is certainly grist for the social studies mill. Knowing who owns which media and whether ownership is influential in reporting the news is not only of interest to secondary social studies students, but the American citizenry, as well. Here are two Web sites that will allow students to view newspapers and news magazines from every state in the United States and from many other countries:

- The *Columbia Review:* http://www.cjr.org/
- *Newslink:* http://newslink.org/

Research tools on these sites will enable students to engage in interesting investigations.

The ability to find information is the crux of technological literacy for students in secondary schools. A helpful Web site, composed by a technical "guru" (http://www.sree.net/stories/web.html), will provide most students and teachers with everything they need to become technologically literate, skillful, and capable of "smart surfing."

Notes

[1] Adapted from Christine J. Yeh & Christopher Drost (2000), *Bridging Identities Among Ethnic Minority Youth in Schools* (ED462511 2002-02-00). ERIC Digest.

[2] Adapted from Pat Beckman (2001), *Access to the General Education Curriculum for Students with Disabilities* (ED458735 2001-10-00), ERIC Clearinghouse on Disabilities and Gifted Education (ERIC EC).

[3] Adapted from Evelyn Holt Otten (2000), *Character Education* (ED444932 2000-09-00). ERIC Digest.

References

Beauchamp, George A. (1964). *The Curriculum of the elementary school.* Boston: Allyn and Bacon.

Beckman, Pat. (2001). *Access to the Curriculum for students with disabilities* (ED 458735 2001-10-00). ERIC Clearinghouse on Disabilities and Gifted Education (ERIC EC) http://ericec.org/digests/e615.html). Accessed March 7, 2006.

Bloom, B., Englehart, M., Furst, E., Hill, W., & Krathwohl, O. (1953). *Taxonomy of educational objectives: The classification of educational goals: Handbook 1. The cognitive domain.* White Plains, NY: Longman.

Boeree, C. George. (2006). *Abraham Maslow.* Available: http://www.ship.edu/~cgboeree/maslow.html (accessed April 7, 2006).

Boston, Carol. (2001). *The debate over national testing* (ED458214 2001-04-00). ERIC Digest. Available: http://www.ericdigests.org/2002-2/testing.htm (accessed April 7, 2006).

Bourne, Alec. (ND). The quotations page. From *Michael Moneur's cynical quotations.* Available: http://www.quotationspage.com (accessed March 3, 2006).

Brown, Elmer E. (1926). *The making of our middle school.* New York: Longman.

Burden, Paul R., & Byrd, David M. (2003). *Methods of effective teaching Teaching*, pp. 222–223. Boston: Allyn & Bacon.

Canter, Lee. (1992). *Lee Canter's assertive discipline: Secondary workbook, grades 9–12.* Bloomington, IN: Solution Tree.

Churchward, Budd. (2003). *The Honor Level System: Discipline by Design.* Available: http://www.honorlevel.com (accessed April 4, 2006).

Cremin, L. A. (1982). *American education: The national experience, 1783–1876.* New York: Harper & Row.

Cubberley, Ellwood P. (1947). *Public education in the United States.* Boston: Houghton Mifflin.

Engle, Shirley H. (1949). Controversial Issues in World History Classes. In Edith West, ed., *Improving the teaching of world history.* Washington, DC: National Council for the Social Studies.

Ford, Paul L. (1897). *The New England Primer: A history of its origins and development*, rev. ed. New York: Dodd, Mead.

Gardner, Howard. (1983). *Frames of mind.* Boston: Harvard University Press.

Gordon, Thomas. (2003). *Teacher effectiveness training: The program proven to help teachers bring out the best in students of all ages.* New York: Three Rivers Press/Crown Publications Group (div. of Random House). Available: http://www.gordontraining.com (accessed March 7, 2006).

Herbart, Johann F. (1894). *Textbook of psychology.* New York: Appleton.

Houlihan, G. Thomas. (2005). *"A View from the Nation's Capitol,"* presentation at the 3rd Annual National School Conference Institute, July 2005. Available: http://www.ccsso.org/about_the_council/leadership_team/index.cfm (accessed April 3, 2006).

The John Dewey Project on Progressive Education, *A Brief Overview of Progressive Education*. College of Education & Social Sciences, The University of Vermont. Available: http://www.uvm.edu/~dewey/articles/proged.html (accessed April 24, 2006).

Johnson, James A., Dupuis, Victory L., Musial, Diann, Hall, Gene E., & Gollnick, Donna M. (1999). *Introduction to the foundations of American education*. Boston: Allyn and Bacon.

Kauchak, D. & Eggen, P. (1998). *Learning & teaching: Research-based methods,* 3rd ed. Boston: Allyn and Bacon.

Kliebard, Herbert M. (1992). Constructing a history of the American curriculum. In Philip W. Jackson, ed., *Handbook of research on curriculum*. pp. 157–184. New York: Macmillan.

Knight, Edgar W. (1951). *Education in the United States.* 3rd ed. Boston: Ginn.

Lumsden, Linda (1997, July). *Expectations for students* (ED409609). ERIC Digest. Available: http://cepm.uoregon.edu/publications/digests/digest116.html (accessed April 7, 2006).

McDaniel, Thomas R. (1986). A Primer on Classroom Discipline: Principles Old and New. *Phi Delta Kappan 68* (1), 63–67.

Monetti, David M., & Hinkle, Terry T. (2003). *Five important test interpretation skills for school counselors* (ED481472). ERIC Digest. Available: http://www.ericdigests.org/2005-2/counselors.html (accessed April 7, 2006).

Monroe, Paul. (1940). *Founding of the American public school system*. New York: Macmillan.

Moskal, Barbara M. (2003). *Developing classroom performance assessments and scoring* (ED481714 2003-06-00). ERIC Digest. Available: http://www.ericdigests.org/2005-2/scoring.html (accessed April 7, 2006).

National Council for the Social Studies. (1989). Report of the Ad Hoc Committee on Scope and Sequence, 1988. *Social Education 53*(6): 375. Washington, DC: Authors

Ornstein, Allan C., & Hunkins, Francis P. (1998). *Curriculum foundations, principles, and issues.* Boston: Allyn and Bacon.

Ornstein, Allan C., & Levine, Daniel U. (1993). *An Introduction to the foundations of education,* 5th ed. Boston: Houghton Mifflin.

Otten, Evelyn Holt. (2000). *Character education* (ED444932 2000-09-00). Eric Clearinghouse for Social Studies/Social Science Education: http://www.hi-ho.ne.jp/taku77/refer/444932.htm (accessed April 7, 2006).

Piaget, J. (1977). *The development of thought: Equilibrium of cognitive structures.* New York: Viking Press.

Pinar, William F., Reynolds, William M., Slattery, Patrick, & Taubman, Peter M. (1995). *Understanding curriculum.* New York: Peter Lang.

Potts, Bonnie. (1994). Strategies for teaching critical thinking. *Practical Assessment, Research & Evaluation*, 4(3). Available: http://PAREonline.net/getvn.asp?v=4&n=3 (Accessed April 24, 2006).

The Project for Excellence in Journalism. (2005). *The State of the News Media 2005: An Annual Report on American Journalism.* Available: http://www.stateofthemedia.com/2005/narrative_overview_intro.asp?cat=1&media=1 (accessed April 7, 2006).

Raubinger, F. M., Rowe, H. G., Piper, D. L., & West, C. K. (1969). *The development of secondary education.* New York: Macmillan.

Rush, Benjamin. (1786). *A plan for the establishment of public schools.* Philadelphia: Thomas Dobson.

Schreyer Institute for Teaching Excellence. (1992). *Teaching by discussion.* Available: http://www.schreyerinstitute.psu.edu (accessed April 7, 2006)

Skeel, Dorothy J. (1995). *Elementary social studies—Challenges for tomorrow's world.* Belmont, CA: Wadsworth.

Spring, Joel. (1990). *The American school: 1642–1990.* New York: Longman.

Stockard, James W. (2003). *Activities for elementary school social studies,* 2nd ed. Long Grove, IL: Waveland Press.

Travers, P., & Rebore, R. (1990). *Foundations of education: Becoming a teacher.* Englewood Cliffs, NJ: Prentice Hall.

Yeh, Christine J., & Drost, Christopher. (2002). *Bridging identities among ethnic minority youth in schools* (ED462511 2002-02-00). ERIC Digest.

Young, E. (1999). *Innovations in earth sciences.* Santa Barbara, CA: ABC-CLIO.

Westerhoff, John H. (1978). *McGuffey and his readers: Piety, morality, and education in nineteenth century America*. Nashville, TN: Abingdon.

Wong, Harry, & Rosemary T. Wong. (2004). *The first days of school: How to be an effective teacher.* Mountain View, CA: Harry Wong Publications, Inc. Available: http://www.harrywong.com (accessed March 7, 2006).

Index